Mending Ourselves

Expressions of healing
& self-integration

Many Voices Press
PO Box 2639
Cincinnati, OH
45201-2639

1993

Mending Ourselves
Expressions of healing & self-integration
By the readers of MANY VOICES
Edited by Lynn W.

Published by
MANY VOICES PRESS
PO Box 2639
Cincinnati, OH 45201-2639

ISBN 0-9637277-0-2

This publication is intended as an information exchange only. It is sold with the understanding that the publisher is not engaged in rendering medical or psychotherapeutic service. Competent professionals in the field of dissociative disorders should be consulted for authoritative treatment and advice.

Printed in the United States of America

Front cover art by Kaye K.
Frontspiece & back cover art by Mary S.

Table of Contents

Chapter 3 Fighting the Good Fight
Persistence in the face of pain **81**

Chapter 4 Moving Closer
Maybe there's hope after all. **113**

Chapter 5 Stories of Integration
On the brink of recovery **149**

Chapter 6 Parables of Healing
Once upon a time... 211

Chapter 7 Afterglow
Living in the light 249

♋

Acknowledgments

I would like to thank the following friends and associates for their unique contributions and support as this book was prepared: Louis Birner, Ph.D., Lilia Brady, Max Burkhardt, David Garling, M.D., Carl Gandola, Lana Giller, Donna Hoffman, Clare Walsh Johnson, Mark Palm and the folks at Micro One, Bill Taylor, Caroline Totten, Dick Westfall, Diane M. Vickery, M.D., and the MV coloring party volunteers: Alice, Debbie, Eleanor, Kaye, Linda, Pam, Sally, Susan and others.

Also, unlimited appreciation to the readers and contributors of MANY VOICES, and the members of the *International Society for the Study of Multiple Personality and Dissociation* who have taught me so much.

Without your help, this book would not exist.

MENDING OURSELVES is dedicated to Diane and Jim Wasnak, with love.

Lynn W., Editor

8/26/93

Editor's Remarks

During the year-long course of this project, I've been privileged to review hundreds of contributions for this book, each coming from a special, deep part of the recovering person. It has been a rewarding emotional experience for me. The choices for publication were difficult to make. I aimed for a cross-section of styles and abilities, offering material relevant to people in all stages of recovery.

The collection includes many different approaches and attitudes toward the processes of healing, and what "integration" really means. Particularly in the *Stories of Integration* (Chapter 5), some experiences feel chaotic, while others seem more gentle and relaxed. From reading the submissions, I'm not at all sure that survivors have a choice in the way integration happens for them. While a smooth unification may be the ideal, I suspect for most of us, this is a time of momentous change. Such change is rarely calm and uneventful.

But while preparing the book, I spoke directly to a number of people who report "full integration." It is heartening to report that every one of the people I've met is pleased about the experience. There may be some losses, but the rewards of living a more unified, harmonious life seem to far outweigh those losses. These recovering people seem more energetic, more caring of themselves, are able to care for others, and look forward to life regardless of their age. (Some are over 50, and lived decades as persons divided.) Many are actively engaged in pursuing goals and dreams that surfaced during the recovery process, and they are delightfully enthused.

One reminder: though some of our writers describe particular healing techniques and medical regimens that worked for them, this is not to be construed as a treatment recommendation for others. These are reported effects, and do not constitute medical advice. Anyone with a severe abuse history should be in treatment or close communication with appropriate health care professionals who can guide them to the individualized help they need. Books can be very useful adjuncts, but nothing takes the place of a competent therapist. If you have or think you have a dissociative disorder, don't cheat yourself of health by trying to bypass therapy. It is easy to wind up in abusing situations, or re-abusing yourself.

These precautions aside — I hope you find the following pages as reassuring and enlightening as I did.

Lynn W.

Foreword

Pros and Cons of Integration

By Nancy G. Burns, Psy.D., and "#1"

Recently, the person I have worked the longest with — five and a-half years — and the first person I diagnosed with Multiple Personality Disorder, asked me to share with her the pros and cons of integration. She also asked for help to understand the "dumb shit" things she does and to explain that to her and her significant other. "#1," as she is affectionately thought of, has taught me more about psychotherapy and dissociation than any other person. She has also taught me a lot about myself.

The following are ideas we generated through our work together. They are shared with you, the reader, in the hopes that they will further your own process of integration and hasten your achievement of your fullest potential as a human person. Successful growth, development,and integration as a human being depends on strengths, willpower, and hope. We wish you all healthy living.

PROS:

1) Integration allows you to focus your strengths so that you can use your skills, tools, knowledge, energy and overall perspective to problem-solve, think, direct behaviors and set and achieve goals. In other words, integration allows you to be more effective in daily living.

2) Integration allows you to assess a situation, relationship, or problem on various dimensions simultaneously and to consciously direct your behavior accordingly.

3) Integration allows you to combine your cognitive, spiritual, and innate intelligences to direct and orchestrate your actions.

4) Integration allows you to understand the process of interactions within interpersonal relationships so that you can make clear choices about the boundaries you need to feel safe and secure.

5) Integration also allows you to understand how the past, present, and future interact.

6) Integration allows you to have better access to the stored memories of your mind. It allows you to flow smoothly through time across variable levels of consciousness each day.

7) Integration allows you to achieve a continuous memory and an ability to comprehend life more fully.

8) Integration allows you more choices, more control, more responsibility for your life.

9) Integration is a form of mastery. As a patient in therapy, integration is typically viewed as a success, an accomplishment and a peak experience in life. A window, as it were, to another plane of existence.

10) Finally, integration is perhaps a step towards spiritual harmony. The clarity of focus, direction of will and intuitive correctness of integrated thinking could be thought of as the closest thing to God-in-self most people will ever achieve.

CONS:

1) Integration may cause you to feel more. You will feel all of your feelings, all of the time.

2) Integration takes away from your ability to compartmentalize, especially automatically.

3) Integration will decrease your tolerance for hate, pain, fear, violence and depression.

4) Integration will take away the valid excuse of poor memory or amnesia.

5) Integration will force you to accept the truth about your past, yourself, and the world around you.

6) Integration will reduce your tolerance for drugs.

7) Integration will decrease your ability to space out.

8) Integration may lower your hypnotizability.

9) Integration will make your thoughts more complex, full of paradoxes, ambiguities, unknowns, and mysteries.

10) Integration will take you closer to the end of your close relationship with your therapist, and will force you to grieve and face the life ahead of you.

Chapter

1

Beginning Awareness

Something is wrong! What can I do?

Daring

When you reflect upon the topic, *mending ourselves*, it is a mystery. A lot of what-if's surround it. Or yet again — *can I do's*.
Then the darting dares...

Oh, you want to see the mystery that is in the box so bad, it's all you can think of as a dare darts by. The air glittering around the mystery box.

Another brightly glowing dare darts by and almost lands on your nose. You think *I must*.

So you reach out, touch the box. Doubts arise.

What if I'm not strong enough?.

You look within. The mystery box is empty. Only a mirror on the floor.

Then you know the answer to the mystery box. The strength to mend came from within you...all your work, your soul joy full...
for in the end no doctors or therapists can heal you. That's the mystery between you and God, and each new day.

You replace the cover...as a young woman timidly walks toward the mystery box. You feel a warm glow engulf you as you stand and watch. *She's in good hands*, you think. *He got me through to the mystery box. He'll do for her, too.*

Now I'm a helper along the path to the mystery box, with the warm glow around me.

By PEG in STACY JOY

♋

Beginnings

You hold everything —
the memories the
feelings.
the clouds hold the water
that must become the rain.

To end this winter
The rain must fall
in torrents
with thunder &
lightning,
pounding,
flooding.

i am so afraid.
i know you are too.

but it is only after that storm
that the sun can finally shine
on our icy landscape,
that spring can come to us.

and i hope
i hope
there will be flowers.

By Megan

♋

Betrayal

By FRIENDS OF ANGELA

Beaten, broken, battered, blue you must always live the lie. Always smiling, pretending nothing's wrong; for you see if you tell, people won't understand you. "People will call you crazy," say the parents. Listening, living the lies, not knowing better — all families live like this, surely. Believing all you hear, for parents surely can't be wrong. Big people don't lie.

One day you find yourself carrying on the abuse, the parents long gone. Betrayed by all before you. Relatives, teachers, other adults looking the other way or causing you more damage. The hurt is there. The pain lingers on, but the ultimate betrayal is to yourself. Betrayed by your own fears. Betrayed by still playing parent tapes through your head, following messages that were wrong from the start. Betrayed by continuing the pain, to cause injury to the body — which is innocent, and always was.

You can't do anything about the past, but you can change the present. The pain must end. The abuse must stop. The only betrayal you can change is to yourself. Learn to take care of you. You really are a special person, capable of great love.

♋

Down Underneath

I've worn a mask all my life
Different masks
Yet all masks just the same
One's of a life that never truly existed
A mask of no pain — no feelings
The mask of a good child
A perfect child
But there were feelings — there was pain
As I grew older
The masks became easier to put on
For I had learned early
How to put on all the masks
To hide — to exist only on the ceiling
How to escape the pain — the feelings caused by abuse
To become the perfect adult — yet an oh-so-damaged one
Where were the feelings — the pain
Down Underneath
Where the damage is!

By C.L.B. and the Orchestra

♋

Currents within.
By Sue K.

Depth

How can I feel when there is no feeling
How can I see what isn't there
How can I cry when there's no emotion
How can I love when my heart doesn't care ...

By J. Team

Abuse imprisons. Grief releases. Expression heals. Abuse imprisons
Grief releases. Expression heals. Abuse imprisons. Grief releases
Expression heals. Abuse imprisons. Grief releases. Expression heals
Abuse imprisons. Grief releases. Expression heals. Abuse imprisons
Grief releases. Expression heals. Abuse imprisons. Grief releases
Expression heals. Abuse imprisons. Grief releases. Expression heals
Abuse imprisons. Grief releases. Expression heals. Abuse imprisons
Grief releases. Expression heals. Abuse imprisons. Grief releases
Expression heals. Abuse imprisons. Grief releases. Expression heals
Abuse imprisons. Grief releases. Expression heals. Abuse imprisons
Grief releases. Expression heals. Abuse imprisons. Grief releases
Expression heals. Abuse imprisons. Grief releases. Expression heals
Abuse imprisons. Grief releases. Expression heals. Abuse imprisons
Grief releases. Expression heals. Abuse imprisons. Grief releases
Expression heals. Abuse imprisons. Grief releases. Expression heals
Abuse imprisons. Grief releases. Expression heals. Abuse imprisons
Grief releases. Expression heals. Abuse imprisons. Grief releases
Expression heals. Abuse imprisons. Grief releases. Expression heals
Abuse imprisons. Grief releases. Expression heals. Abuse imprisons
Grief releases. Expression heals. Abuse imprisons. Grief releases
Expression heals. Abuse imprisons. Grief releases. Expression heals
Abuse imprisons. Grief releases. Expression heals. Abuse imprisons
Grief releases. Expression heals. Abuse imprisons. Grief releases
Expression heals. Abuse imprisons. Grief releases. Expression heals
Abuse imprisons. Grief releases. Expression heals. Abuse imprisons
Grief releases. Expression heals. Abuse imprisons. Grief releases
Expression heals. Abuse imprisons. Grief releases. Expression heals
Abuse imprisons. Grief releases. Expression heals. Abuse imprisons
Grief releases. Expression heals. Abuse imprisons. Grief releases
Expression heals. Abuse imprisons. Grief releases. Expression heals
Abuse imprisons. Grief releases. Expression heals. Abuse imprisons
Grief releases. Expression heals. Abuse imprisons. Grief releases
Expression heals. Abuse imprisons. Grief releases. Expression heals
Abuse imprisons. Grief releases. Expression heals. Abuse imprisons
Grief releases. Expression heals. Abuse imprisons. Grief releases
Expression heals. Abuse imprisons. Grief releases. Expression heals
Abuse imprisons. Grief releases. Expression heals. Abuse imprisons
Grief releases. Expression heals. Abuse imprisons. Grief releases
Expression heals. Abuse imprisons. Grief releases. Expression heals
Abuse imprisons. Grief releases. Expression heals. Abuse imprisons
Grief releases. Expression heals. Abuse imprisons. Grief releases
Expression heals. Abuse imprisons. Grief releases. Expression heals

By Daile

Status Report

It's not about incest anymore

it's about dissociative disorders
identifying parts
co-consciousness and integration

it's about host personalities
alters who threaten, who scream, who protect, who write
a person lost somewhere in the twilight zone

it's about telling secrets
coming out of hiding
facing the truth
having feelings

it's about love and hurt all mixed together
anxiety and lots of it
nightmares and flashbacks

it's about migraine headaches and internal battles
keeping my feet on the ground
managing new medications
trying to appear normal

it's about going away
it's about staying here

it's about children who never grow up
it's about adults who were never children

it's about getting to know myself
finding out there is a name for what I have
finding out I'm not the only one

it's about commitment to getting well
believing in myself
letting someone else take care of me

it's about letting go
it's about being ready
it's about trusting for the first time

By Genie for R. Nichamin &Co.

♋

Voices

There are tears unspoken
voices unheard
walks down paths
lined with weeds
battered roses
and broken crosses
memories
seen
and unseen
hope hidden
under layers of pain
and fear
uncovered
in ordinary days
and rare moments
of tranquility
Terror shrouding a life
struggling to maintain
some sense of normalcy
teetering on the edge
of a tunnel
often visited
always black and endless
There are voices speaking now
some hesitant and soft
some insistent and harsh
some expressed in
crayon and pencil
symbols
splashes of paint
or the voices of others
All afraid
reluctant to trust
and needing to be
joined together
by a thread of hope
and a determination
to continue the healing
of a butterfly

seeking simply
a safe place
to exercise her wings
as she flies toward
ordinary days
    and nights
filled with
friendly shadows
and a rising sun.

By Janice S.

Talking Together
By Beth Gassen-Parsons

Inner Children

Quivering inside, growing weaker as time treads by
   Silently pursuing truth
What is truth? By whose authority is it decided?
   Who really knows?
The voices of the inner children know
   but they are silenced by the Fearsome One
To say more is to invite death and destruction
   as surely as one dealt with the Devil himself.
Yet the silencing menace, the Fearsome One
   hesitates, on the brink of discovery, now unsure
Could the voices be real: the pain of the children?
   Or are her defenses merely weakening?

Deep inside the sound of children crying, begging.
   "Do not leave us in our prison of memories.
We have seen a glimpse of hope and cannot survive
   without acknowledgment, without unconditional love.
Our voices grow weaker, our strength vanishing
   into the black hole of our despair.
Why won't you listen, give heed to our words?
   We are real and our stories must be heard."

The Keeper of the Memories, always guarding
   Stubbornly refusing to hear the sad cries
Briefly hesitates, pausing to wonder
   Could it be? Could she be wrong?
But "wrong" would affect a lifetime of pictures
   The fantasy world created in her mind
Could she stand to face that, to know truth
   Or would the pain be more than she could stand?
Wilting, slithering to the ground like a red rose dying
   Fading into nothingness, forlorn, lost.
Can this be the fate of the children
   who have waited so patiently to be believed?

"Believe us, please, we have no reason to lie
   No reason to make up horrendous hurts
Believe us, trust us, you're our only hope
   for freedom from this dark dungeon of death."

"We've kept most of the memories for many long years,
    awaiting the time we could tell.
Now that we've started, we want to tell all
    the secrets that are eating us alive."

"There are monsters and dragons and
    snakes in our dungeon
They will get us because we dared speak
    Unless you can save us from all that we fear
By believing the words that we say."

"We wish it were different. We all wanted love.
    Not to be tortured and then tossed away.
But the love that was given was tainted, unpure.
    We view the parade of memories, alone."

"Why do you continue to abuse us, to hurt
    in the name of love?
All we ask is that you trust us, believe what we say.
    We need unconditional love."

"Love that doesn't care if we make mistakes,
    or if we don't do things the way you want us to.
Love that will hold us, protect us from them,
    and always acknowledge our value."

"We are valuable, your children within.
    We hold memories that can unlock the door.
But if you fight against us, deny our thoughts,
    We will curl up like a starving baby; we won't survive."

A baby cannot survive without sustenance for her soul
    Else she will crawl off the edge of the world and die.
A baby needs love, kindness and warmth.
    Be a parent to your inner children.

By Paula Jamison

♋

What Do I Want?

answers
feelings
      to make it all go away
      to be normal
      to be free
      to be whole
      to get out of bed in the morning
      to fall asleep at night
      to dream without nightmares
      to be at peace

By Genie for R. Nichamin & Co.

♋

Braided Forms
By Sue K.

The Essence of Recovery

By PATRICK, One of Many

We are many yet we are one. With only two years in therapy, we have already faced many of the challenges of recovery. Cooperation is one of our greatest obstacles. Thanks to our therapist though, we are all beginning to understand its necessity.

One of the primary tools we have to aid in this challenge of collaboration is the computer. Thanks to this box of modern technology, many of us are able to express ourselves in writings. For some, it is merely a form of communication between each other. For others, such as myself, it is a link to the outside, a creative release for pent-up emotions, both positive as well as negative.

Instead of pulling apart in our own directions, we now are better able to work together. Like a unique computerized system, we are all linked together by our main "host."

Individually we contribute to the input as well as output. As a general rule things run smoothly. However, there are times when we experience those exasperating "ERROR" messages and even an occasional "CRASH."

When this malfunction occurs, we older ones have learned to avoid panic. We work collectively to not only restore the system but also to analyze what caused this breakdown, and what steps can be taken to prevent a recurrence.

We are not always successful in our efforts, but even though we may experience failure, we do so in a unified endeavor. This is the essence of Recovery.

♋

Self-Protection

I built my turrets
when I was small:
layers of personalities
to ward off the foe
who was my family.

One shielded me from pain;
one, from abandonment;
one from certain tears;
one from rape;
all, from memories.

Now I need no such walls
and must tear down the turrets
without destroying those pieces
who are not a part of me,
yet are.

By Rosemarie B. Wendt

♋

Life

When the rubble
caused by a disaster
Is finally swept away...
what's left except a disaster area.
When the pieces of a broken life
are finally in full view
Nakedness is all that's left...
to see and turn from
Not wanting to see another's
pain...
afraid you'll see your own.
Life's been a disaster area for me
with rubble scattered here to
there.
Rubble created by many...
Swept away by none...
till now.
For now I've begun the Re-building,
the piecing
together of the major disaster area
I call life.

By C.L.B. and the Orchestra

♋

The sum of my parts.
By Mary Jane

A Thousand Miles From Everyone

By ALEX & SORRIE
(We, along with the rest of the gang, live inside Joyce.)

When we open the shades in the morning
everything looks as though it's upside down and inside out.
The sky seems green, the grass seems blue.
People are walking by our window on their heads.
The buildings in the distance are standing upside down —
their offices outside — their windows inside.
The coffee brews backwards, the toaster cools the toast.
Our head feels as though it's traveling a hundred miles a minute
in complete and incomplete circles.
We get dizzy from all the confusion.
But no one is allowed to tell. We must do this alone.
Alone is how we feel.
So many people inside — yet ever so alone.
One people seem to be able to get their needs met
and stay on track.
When you're as many as we are,
no one ever knows what's going on.
Everything moves very fast.
How did we get here? Who got dressed?
Who holds the feelings today?
We know people look at us and see our deep confusion
 — but how do we hide it?
Everyone is so out of control.
We can't keep friends
because everyone always has a different opinion.
Some of us get hurt easily, some not at all.
Quiet — don't tell!
Everyone else is much more important.
Never ever tell. We don't need anyone.
People seem to walk in and out a revolving door in our lives
for we hear what they say to us upside down and inside out.
Does anyone out there understand what it feels like to know
someone is talking in English but you hear them in French?
The panic sets in.
Who is it? What do they want?
Quiet! No one tell anyone.
Hide in the closet, little ones. It'll go away.

Years have gone by...has it stopped?
No, only worsened.
Trust someone, the outsiders tell us.
We try — we get hurt. Trust becomes harder.
Broken promises, broken hearts, broken bones.
It's OK. That means the outsiders like us.
Outsiders think we forget when told promises — but we don't.
We put them in our promise box for all to read.
Some have pictures so the little ones could read them.
Can one person understand many? We can't understand one.
Quiet! Don't talk!
Everyone is more important.
Their problems hurt more.
They need more help and attention from others.
Quiet please. Don't be seen. Don't be heard.
No one will love us anyway.
There's too many of us. Who would ever understand?
Go, little ones and big alike.
Hide in the closet; it's safe there.
No one will look for you. No one will love you.
Quiet, please. Stop your heart from hurting.
There is no one there to hold you.
It's all too much.
Quiet, please.

♋

The Dilemma of the Seed

By the TEAM
for Sleeping Judy, the original child

I am surrounded by dark.

The ground that I'm buried in keeps me warm. With just enough water and oxygen to survive, I exist. I am alone, but my needs are being met.

There's talk of something called light, rain, air, and others like me, but it takes a lot of work to get there. I'll have to push real hard and break through the very shell that has protected me. The ground will push back without effort. There's so much of it, but I'm used to it, don't even notice it. What will it be like out of my shell, out of my warm dirt? Will there really be others like me, or will I be alone, tricked?

Does the sun hurt? Will it burn me? Can I adjust to the brightness? I'm warm now, warm in my darkness. How could this new way be better? Does the rain know when to stop? Will I get too much, and drown among the refreshing rain drops? I get enough water now, most of the time. Sometimes I get a little dry because no one sees me and they forget, but that's okay. I just have to depend on the water that squeezes through. What about air? There is pollution. I might choke or not be used to so much oxygen, and get dizzy and over-whelmed.

There's so much to change in order to survive sprouthood. Growing and reaching out is so different than sitting and absorbing. What will I do? What if it's all a lie? How do I know when I break through if I will be okay? What if there's nothing there? At least I'm familiar with the nothing I have now.

♋

Vision

Seeing more than
how to
make up--create
real people
out of nothing,
but the sheer need
to escape.

New Vision

Whole, not divided
Imagining life

dots of light forming
petaled pools of intense creation

Giving birth into a new season,
the shadowed self taking down walls
walking into vision.
Each of us holding hands
our essence captured like the fresh rain
that makes up the puddle.

Vision.
The beginning
of
collective
time.

By Kathy R.

♋

A New Year

By KATHY RUIZ

- January 1, 1993

What a New Year! My New Year's Eve was a confusing, terrifying and cathartic night.

I want very much to tell this tale. It seems almost unbelievable.

It began with my usual feeling of fear and the familiar sense of impending doom. Someone inside transferred her thoughts of self-mutilation to my consciousness. They persisted again and again. *Get the scissors* she yells, over and over.

I do get the scissors, and a needle. I don't want to, but I can't stop it either. I watch as someone takes the scissors and cuts. The scissors are put down. The needle is picked up. The needle jabs. I watch all this. I can't stop it.

I cry inside, *I want my doctor!* I reach for the phone. I'm ashamed to call him. Instead I phone a crisis counselor at the local hospital's mental health unit. I tell him my first name; we talk. He later asks me if I have a doctor. I tell him I do and who he is. Well, thirty minutes later my doctor calls. I guess he really does care about me.

He asks me to go inside. Meet the others face to face. Tell them how I feel about their actions. Ask the others to stop this hurtful behavior. I agree to try.

I go inside. I see the hooded one. I believe the hooded one is a man and a helper. He has me floating above the ground. He asks me to lie down in the air, suspended. He, the hooded one, has the control. He is conducting the transformation.

As I lie in the air, I see the others approaching. First, Pricilla followed by Marie and the Baby. My stomach outlined in a balloon shape as if pregnant. Slowly, one by one, they each enter this space, this hole. They fit as puzzle shapes, each connecting to each other, and then to me.

I feel so calm, so peaceful, almost euphoric. I begin to cry. All their pain, all their memories begin popping in my head. They are racing by so fast. I don't recognize some of the scenes or some of the faces. I suppose it will all make sense in time.

This event was so magical, so mystical. There isn't a soul on earth, other than my doctor and me who would ever believe it. (And I wonder what my doctor really thinks and feels about this event.)

I've neglected to mention that there were two others attending — my Teenager and Little Kathy — in addition to the hooded one. As this catharsis was happening, the Teenager and Little Kathy watched. They showed no outward signs of emotion. I can only imagine what they were thinking.

After my doctor and I hung up (at 8:55 p.m.),I lost time. The next thing I realized, I was sitting on my bed in my night clothes, and it was 10:57 p.m. I wondered briefly how I got there and then remembered talking with my doctor. I soon fell asleep.

This morning when I woke, I went downstairs to make coffee. On the kitchen counter were *four* wrappers from ice-cream sandwiches, and an entire used foil of laxatives. My delight at having "integrated" three of my alters was quickly deflated by the revelation that the two remaining are my most independent and distrustful. I believe this scene was my Teenager's way of communicating to me: *I am still here and can control the body whenever I want.*

OK, so I'm humbled. I'm still a multiple. Let's just keep this a secret from those remaining inside, about how happy I am.

♋

The Moment

This is the moment
can we say it
Can we divulge our secrets
Do we dare show we know
where the Pain comes from?
Can we say to our therapist
We see the storm's origin
We feel the vicious beats
We know they seek to smash
us against — what rocks?
The rocks of our own Souls.
We are the ones who beat
and rage
The storms we see
are within us.
Can you let us know
the gentleness you show
when we let you.
Can you give us grace
to try again?

By The Committee

♋

The Secret Pain

From a place buried deep, it comes.
It comes and I cannot run.
Feet dragging, heavy and relentless,
It mounts the stairs.

I hear it first. Then smell it.
Then see it. Then taste it.
Then — frozen with fear — I feel it.

I feel it, the secret pain.
Then I *am* the pain.
Fire and ice course through my blood,
Wracking each nerve with memories, memories.

God, I have sinned against others.
I have sinned against myself.
And I have sinned against you.
But please take pity.

Drag this beast off my back
And send it hurtling down, down,
Deep to that secret place
And lock it there
And keep it from me.

For that's the only way I can live.

God?

By Deb, Etc.

♋

The pain in my heart wrenches my soul
*   ...and I am not whole*

By Emily of KGP

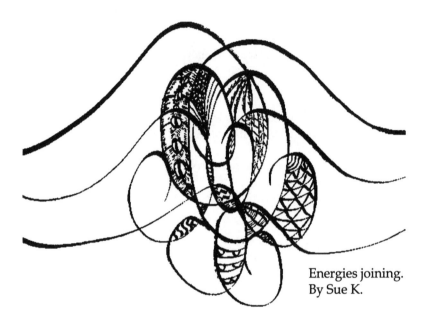

Energies joining.
By Sue K.

Only A Child

A child
overwhelmed
confused
immobilized
in an incomprehensible world
Scared of being alone
terrified of people
in need of so much nurturing
and a safe place to play

By Lisa

I wish there was a red thread to connect us together and make us one.

By Rachael

♋

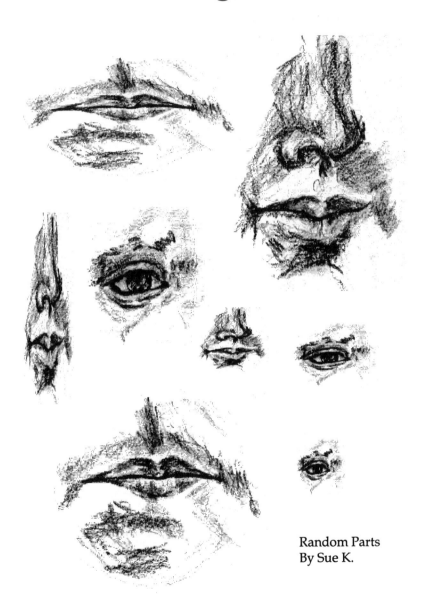

Random Parts
By Sue K.

Masks

What mask will I wear today -- the good or the bad?
  Or maybe it's best to hide behind the lost and the sad.
Sometimes it's hard to decide which one to wear today.
  They're each one waiting to come and be in my play.

I look at others around me and I watch them to see
  What do I do; oh, they'll show me how to be.
That's how I've lived in this life of pain so long
  That's how I could pretend; that's how I was so strong.

Can you hear me screaming?
  Do you see my tears streaming?
Whoever's out there, please grab my hand
  I'm falling down fast and I can hardly stand.

First I say I'm good and then I say I'm bad.
  It's a constant battle now and I feel so very sad.
I'm tired of fighting and I'm out of rhyme or reason
  It feels like the time has come to end my life's season.

But once more I'll scream out in anguish and pain
  Over life's treacherous, rugged terrain.

Can you hear me screaming?
  Do you see my tears streaming?
Help me, please help me — I'm here!

By Samantha (in Stephanie's System)

♋

Real

Hole in my soul, hole in my veins.
Hole in my spirit, hole in my brain.
Hole in my joy and hole in my pain.
Sometimes I think I'm going insane.
Hole in my heart, hole in my hand.
Hole when I sit, hole when I stand.
It's something I can't even understand.

Disconnect, separate — exclude it all, d/i/s/s/o/c/i/a/t/e.
Quarantine, isolate — ignore yourself and segregate.
Real is not anything in my mind.
Real is only the daily grind.
Real is now -- not what you left behind.
Real is nothing -- real is gone.
Real is living in Lake Woebegone.
Real is empty -- real is hollow.
Real is something too hard to swallow.
Real is something I just can't follow.

I'm not real, I'm not here.
I'm somewhere up in the atmosphere.
I'm all in pieces — I don't c o n n e c t.
I can't remember but I don't forget.
I'm not the same as those I see.
I've had to live my life so differently.
Their real world is so far from my reality.
They are one but I am a we.

Real will stab, real will cringe.
Real will send your heart on a binge.
Real will twist and real will tear.
Real will keep your mind in a scare.
I'm not real — I'm not true.
I am yellow and then I'm blue.
I do not do as others do.
My life is not real -- it can't be true.
What happens to me doesn't happen to you.
So what's the answer and where is the clue?
Because I want to be real and I want to be new.
But can a teddy bear suddenly become a kangaroo?
I wish I knew...................

By the Tribe of Barb

Wandering

Wandering
amongst
my
selves...

i
he
she
they
we.
Where is the me,
who met the we?

You must
see, hear, experience, acknowledge, believe, accept
and
trust
they say.

We must
let go...
they say.

And then,
i
he
she
they
we
will find the way
to me

By Judy

♋

Changes

I've had to turn my life upside down. Everything has jiggled out of place. I suspect some things have fallen completely away.

How do I know how to rearrange the pieces? What goes next to what? Are they arranged by color or in alphabetical order?

Some things have lost their names. How will I ever sort them out so that I can know where they belong?

Will I ever find my treasures, or will I have to search for new ones?

By Judy S.

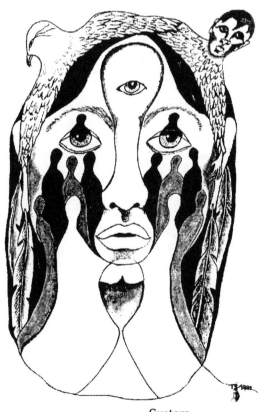

System
By Living Earth

Walking on the Cracks

When a secret rules your life,
you have to live by Secret Rules

By John D.

Being invisible is hard.

You have to learn many things, and then make sure that you *always* do *all* of them correctly; otherwise, something really, really bad will happen to you.

Nobody tells you how to be invisible. You just have to learn by yourself.

Maybe you learn first what makes people see you. You get hurt when they see you, so you must remember what you did that got their attention, and then you try so hard to *never* do it again. Of course, there are many different things that make people notice you, and you have to learn each one — figure out what you did wrong so that they saw you. Then you've got to remember *all* of them. It helps if you can organize them in your mind — then it's easier to check your list before you do or say anything — so that you don't slip up. You can always add to the list.

Maybe after this, you notice that certain situations make people notice you no matter what; so you've got to be ready to escape if you see one of those situations coming. You never know when things will change, so you can never relax. Sometimes a new person will come into the picture. Sometimes it's just the place you're in — or the time of day.   It may be safe one minute but dangerous the next.

So you try to figure out a schedule — what to do/not do; where to be/not be; when is the right time/when is a bad one; who will be where; when; and what will they be doing? And thinking?

Then you've got to keep within your time/place/person/activity slots, or your cover is blown. And you've *got* to be able to see a change coming before it happens, so that you can be elsewhere.

There are always threats to deal with.

Anyone who has hurt you before is always a threat. You avoid them. If you must be in the same time/place/activity slot with them, then you must carefully, meticulously, use all of your active invisibility strategy to cut off interaction with them. This is very tiring, because you are in constant danger and if you goof and get off balance, you are out of the pan and in the fire. Now you've got to go into emergency disarm mode — get their attention away from you and, hopefully, make them forget you. This is very frightening because if it doesn't work, you're a goner. They've got you. (Then what?)

But that's just the people who *already* have hurt you. Everyone else is a potential threat.

So you also have to analyze the people around you. There are some you're around every day. You can nail *their* routines right down tight and dance around them, while walking delicately through the places where your life absolutely, unavoidably, *must* interact with theirs...trying to remain invisible, leaving no lasting impression even as their attention is on you. Then there are those who pop up only occasionally. If you act the right way, say the right thing the right way, most of these will not pay much attention to you. But sometimes, a potential threat turns into a real one.

So you learn to recognize warning signs in people. Certain things may show that some variance from the norm is about to unfold — and that's dangerous to you. It may be a subtle change in voice, body language, speech patterns, silence, a look — many different things. You've got to always be alert to spot these signs right off so that you can flee before the volcano erupts.

It's hard. It takes a lot of time to learn the secret rules. And then, after you've lived by them awhile, you realize that the rules have locked you out of the Human Club. Because, if everyone else can live/talk/laugh/interact, but you can't, there must be something wrong with *you*, right? So you're outside. You don't have a clue as to how to get inside. You're *locked out*.

It's like everyone else can drive on the interstate and get off where they want, but you're stuck walking on the median strip. And there's no exit from the median, and sometimes it disappears completely — *Then* what do you do?

♋

Overwhelming Success

There's a little girl inside of me
who's earned her wings to be set free
despite what her father tries to do
she's made her childhood dreams come true
as her tears have flowed through me
I plant for her a courage tree
her pain now goes where the wild wind blows
success will sound in her future echoes

by Deborah Berding

♋

Wildflowers

Hope --
The flowers God plants
Bloom and grow
Untended
By highways in
Fields and
In sidewalk cracks
Any dirt will do
We don't need much
Nourishment
And don't get much
Except maybe from God.
He is silent Who planted us
But comes quiet in
Sun and rain to sustain us.
We are beautiful to Him maybe
More than all the pansies and
Azaleas that are
Loved in well-planned gardens
By people. But even
On the hottest days and
In the hardest rains
When pansies wilt
We remain,
Swaying a little
In the sun.
Hope --

By Chaunceny of Megan D.

♋

A Private Car

Words and faces crowd and pass.
My mind is a meeting place --
a broad tiled room
that echoes with loud announcements
of the next train,
and the names of those
I am to find and save
from wandering over cold, steel tracks.

Feelings are marked
for consideration later,
like post cards to be sent,
kept on the table in the sun --
addressed to no one I know,
or wish to,
and everyone I've ever met.

This Friday morning,
gray exhaust lays on my eyelids
I cannot sleep to rest.
I run in circles,
searching the still air of the train station.
I send my feelings through the mail.

I just want a private car on this train,
traveling south to warm, west to water.
I'll watch out the window.
Someone will bring me good, hot coffee
and a thick blanket for my legs.
On a tray with flowers I'll find
a new pen and clean, white paper.

Someone will wake me if I fall asleep
so that I do not miss the ocean
cresting in the distance.
And they will bring me post cards
addressed to me in a fine hand,
bidding me home.

By J.W.

Birthings

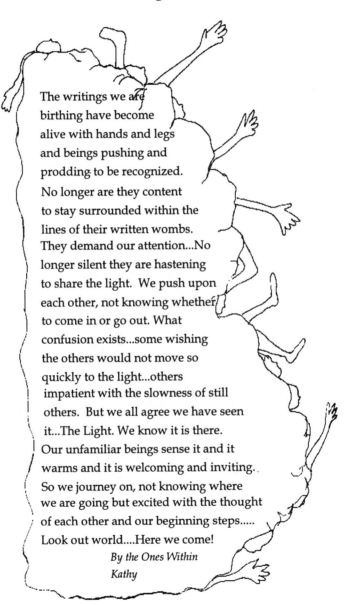

The writings we are
birthing have become
alive with hands and legs
and beings pushing and
prodding to be recognized.
No longer are they content
to stay surrounded within the
lines of their written wombs.
They demand our attention...No
longer silent they are hastening
to share the light. We push upon
each other, not knowing whether
to come in or go out. What
confusion exists...some wishing
the others would not move so
quickly to the light...others
impatient with the slowness of still
others. But we all agree we have seen
it...The Light. We know it is there.
Our unfamiliar beings sense it and it
warms and it is welcoming and inviting..
So we journey on, not knowing where
we are going but excited with the thought
of each other and our beginning steps.....
Look out world....Here we come!

By the Ones Within
Kathy

Flames
By ABB

Chapter

2

Creating Order From Chaos

We begin, and begin again.

Mending Yourself

By CORDUROY

If you have MPD, to begin mending yourself, first you have to know you are broken. You have to be very little — or very desperate — to know you are broken. Prob'ly you will be both.

You don't have to be not scared, but you can't let being scared stop you from working at getting mended.

You have to face it. It is not your fault you are broken. This is very, very hard because it means it's somebody else's fault and you are scared, Scared, SCARED to say or think or feel that somebody you loved hurt you. It's also hard because the big alters keep reading in books and hearing on television that what's wrong with the world is that people don't take responsibility for themselves and just want to blame other people.

Some people inside you say that's what you're doing: being bad and blaming other people for things that are all your fault. When they say this, you need to cover your ears and run away and hide or else you'll prob'ly cut yourself.

If you cut yourself, some people inside will blame you for that, too. It seems you never win with some people inside no matter what you do. (When the body was little, you never could win with the bad people *outside* either, no matter what you did. And that always hurts a whole big bunch.)

You have to find at least one helper to mend yourself and he or she needs to be your therapist. Finding a therapist is hard. Trusting a therapist is harder. Forgiving a therapist when he doesn't know what to do for you to trust him is the hardest of all. But you can't get well by yourself.

For our "family," the *most* important piece of mending ourself is keeping our therapy rules. These are:

#1. We always, Always, ALWAYS make and keep our appointments, no matter what it takes and no matter who (inside *or* outside) pressures us hard not to do it "this time." (If we broke this rule, we would be agreeing that getting mended isn't very important.)

#2. Everybody has to be completely honest with the therapist. You have to say things even if they are embarrassing or shameful or conceited. It is tricky to know what to say because everybody is always thinking of more things than one mouth can say, but if you mean to keep the rule always, you get the hang of how to choose what you're 'sposed to say. Usually.

#3. You have to begin to think of each other as family and start trying to talk to each other. And you have to begin to see why mean alters are that way. At first you don't like those parts! You want to just hate them. You really, Really, REALLY don't want to admit they are part of "YOU." They don't want to admit it, either.

They don't want to admit they're only part of you. They want you to believe their bad ideas are everything there is about you.

#4. If you're ever going to get mended, you have to not kill yourself.

We find this real hard to remember and real hard to do. Lately, our therapist keeps reminding us this a lot. He says our work together is important and it would be a shame to spoil it by dying. We wonder whether a "mended we" will be of enough value to both of us who have worked so hard. He says yes.

#5. You have to learn what things help the people who want to get mended be stronger.

Here are some of our helpers:

1. A best friend. She should be like ours if you can find one. She needs to not lecture you or put you down. She should be strong enough to bear anything you tell her without breaking down herself. (The Librarian says to tell you we believe an MPD or even a depressed person needs to give every close support person permission to have one support person for them that they can talk to so your sickness isn't too hard for them. But you get to approve who they pick since they'll know your secrets. Our best friend has talked to her minister, but not much. Just what she needed to.)

She'll call or come and just love you if you're suicidal or self-destructive and she'll say it's ok (it's not bad, and it's not stupid) that you feel that way, but she doesn't want you to get hurt because she loves you, even when you're out of control.

2. A spiritual director. We guess everybody doesn't have to have this, but ours sure helped me. Without her, I'd still be cowering behind the Father's big chair, longing only to die and afraid to talk to anybody. She's helped a lot of us, but some aren't interested and give the rest of us a hard time about religion, saying how we don't deserve it and we're fake and all of that.

3. Teddy bears are very good to sleep with. But don't be surprised if some morning you wake up and your husband is holding your bear and says he couldn't sleep and you weren't

using it and you always look like it feels so good!

4. Never dress in clothes that make you feel bad.

5. Buy paints and crayons and stuff. Even if you "aren't artistic," sometimes working on drawing what's in your head helps. We call it *giving ourselves art therapy*. Share what you draw with your therapist.

6. Subscribe to *Many Voices*. We never have had a chance to talk to another MPD, so this helps us know we're not crazy and not alone.

7. Keep a journal. We made our sister promise that if we die (in an accident or anything), she would make sure no one in the family ever reads it. We told her that we *had* to know no one would read it so we could write any way we were feeling and we *had* to be able to write whatever we were feeling or it couldn't help us. At first, we tried to hold back some of the worst from the journal, but it slipped in, so we *hope* no one ever reads it. They'd be sorry.
The journal has helped us meet some alters for the first time. It sometimes helps us have conversations together. It helps people know what they think. It can help us work with our therapist, too. A journal is a really, really good thing.

8. Bubble stuff is good because bubbles in the sun are like magic. Going where you can see birds and animals and stuff is magic, too. A big alter says we are trying to say and do things that give a sense of wonder.

9. When things are really bad, it's good to sit in the corner of a small room with the door locked, with a towel or blanket over you. We used to think this was one of the *bad things*, because we were ashamed that it wasn't like normal people. But now we know that since it helps us and doesn't hurt us or anybody else, it's good. But we think we shouldn't do it except when we *really* need to.

10. When you have to be in a public place, sitting against a wall can be comforting. This is weird, too and embarrassing. But it's better to be able to have an ok time in a safer place than to be crawling out of your skin in the middle of the room and maybe come home and hurt yourself. Our real friends help us find good spots to sit and we've learned there are lots of people who look and act normal who prefer these places, too! Watch for them — you'll be surprised.

11. Try to listen to and respect your needs, even if they seem dumb. Let them be important just because they're yours. No-

body listened when you were little, prob'ly, so it's about time, isn't it? (We know some alters will fight you on this, so just do it when you can. Don't let them make you feel guilty when you can't. That's ok. Sometimes not fighting them when you're ex-tra-weak is a need, too).

Do everything you can to help mend yourself. It takes all your work and all your therapist's work and all your support people's work to get well. But in the end, we think only God can really mend you, because only He knows what "you" are supposed to look like. (Should you be integrated? How? Should you be a close- knit family? What pattern should the "stitches" take?)

We don't know why He makes us work so hard at it, and why He takes so long. We think it's very unfair that the people who were most hurt as kids are the same people who have to hurt so much again getting mended. But Julia Mary the Mystic says God isn't making a mistake and someday it will all be worth it. I hope she's right.

Love,

Corduroy (in JMG)
(By the way, Corduroy is an alter whose age *changes*. She can be about 2-3 and hardly able to speak or old as about 7-8, but she still is recognizable as Corduroy. We wonder whether others have alters with changeable ages?)

♋

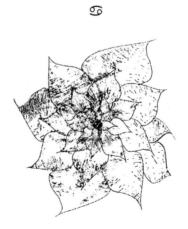

Flowering Inside
By Melissa Burgchardt

Body Care Tips

By KATHY R.

In the past year, we have had a lot of weakness in our body and have felt chronically extremely exhausted. We have taken steps to deal with our health problems and have learned a lot about our body the past six months. The following are things we have learned and wish we knew before. We are glad we know to do these things now:

1. We eat three to six small meals a day to keep our blood sugar levels up, and it has cut down on dissociation about 50 percent. One person might plan the menu, one might shop and one might cook, but no matter how bad anything else is, it gets done. (Eating healthy foods can be a very important grounding technique when processing memories. It helps us keep one foot in the door of the present.)

2. We take multi-vitamins every day, and extra calcium, magnesium, B5 and B6. We believe the calcium and magnesium have helped decrease our intense energy and mental nervousness.

3. We have a good relaxation tape we listen to. This helps us calm down when things are really intense.

4. We go to acupuncture weekly, which has been an enormous benefit. It has helped us get out of the intense "fight or flight loop" our whole system and body was in for many months. At the time, we were feeling old terror 24-hours a day. Because acupuncture balances energy (among many other things), it has been a very good way for people inside to learn about relaxation and to short-circuit some of the intense fight-or-flight body reactions. It has helped the system stop repeating and debilitating energy loops and has helped move things through, rather than 'round and 'round. It has also provided relief from very intense heat we experience in our body when feelings are strong. Some of the heat gets vented now. We can breathe regularly and sleep well most nights now.

5. We brush our skin with a skin brush to help remove accumulated toxins, which we believe have been stored inside our body since the abuse. We try to drink a lot of water too, to help keep things moving.

6. We take natural progesterone made from wild yams to help with the PMS stress. It seems that the body, when out of other stress hormones, converts progesterone into needed stress hormones. It has helped a lot, as has taking vitamin B5, B6, calcium and magnesium, and cutting out caffeine and sugar.

7. We try to get regular exercise, walking 20 minutes to an hour a few times a week, to keep things circulating and help our spirit stay strong.

8. We take herbal formulas that help balance our energy, tonify our blood and strengthen our internal organs.

Slowly, our energy is coming back. As in this whole healing process, sometimes it is two steps forward and one step back. But the list above has helped us immensely. Although it is still hard, we are able to manage things in our life much better. We were on the road to seriously-failing health and instead found a very good acupuncturist who knows a lot about health and nutrition issues. She is our outside body "ally" when we need encouragement.

It has taken a lot of hard work for us to do all the health things that need to be done. But we are really glad about doing it, because it makes us feel better in our body.

♋

Calming Exercise
By Mary

A Declaration
of Independence

By KATIE LOVE MORGAN

In wholeness, September 20, 1991, the unanimous declaration of the thirteen personalities of Kate :

When in the course of maturation, it becomes necessary for an individual to dissolve the ties which have connected her with parents and siblings; and to assume control and responsibility for her own future, a separate and equal standing in society and before God; stepping away from the chains of the past requires that she formally declare this separation.

While children are a gift from God, they are given to parents with certain inalienable rights, and among these are love, respect, and the nurturance of a healthy self-esteem.

Whenever a family unit becomes destructive to these ends, when there have been long periods of neglect and series of abuses, it is the individual's right — it is her duty — to distance herself from such a family; and establish a new one by selectively choosing individuals with whom to form healthy bonds. A foundation for these new relationships should be laid upon God- given principles, by organizing powers and privileges in a way that is most likely to respect the dignity and bring about the fulfillment of all persons concerned.

Such has been the growth processes of our integrated personalities and it is well past the time to separate. Feelings and actions from here forward are no longer bound to the past.

The above withstanding, we can no longer regret that we were not given the love, respect, and nurturance we needed. Parents give love according to their ability at the time. It is crucial to begin to accept our parents' not loving us as a statement about them and not about us. Yet, it is also important to accept that we, as our own person, are not helpless and incapable of affecting changes. We can remove ourselves from unhealthy environments. We can connect with healthy individuals instead. We can choose to associate with individuals who treat us with dignity and respect. We can strive to establish healthy friendships in which there is a mutual exchange of thoughts, feelings, and experiences; healthy relationships in which to express and explore our deepest feelings, hopes, fears, and joys, without fearing condemnation, rejection, or being abandoned. We can form relationships in which we are free to be all that we are, to be comforted, and to gain the strength to continue moving forward.

The solution to this deficit cannot be based solely upon an outside resource, however. A single individual is unable to meet all of our needs. Our heavenly Father is the only One to whom we can turn for every need. God is the kind of Parent a parent should be, and can give us the lasting emotional satisfaction we desire. He is completely able and forever willing to meet our every emotional, physical, and spiritual need if we will just ask Him to walk with us and guide us.

Now is the time to focus attention on our *deepest* heritage. We need to treat ourselves with the same respect God has for us. We were created in His image. The truest thing about us is what He thinks about us. He has already established our worth; and no one — no matter how influential they are in our lives — can nullify what He has done. He has accepted us where we are, and will work with us until we are able to see ourselves as He sees us and until we know Him as He truly is.

We cannot change the circumstances of our birth. But with the help of God and those individuals He brings into our lives, we can change our attitude toward them. We have been through a certain combination of experiences for a purpose. We must use experience, not as a justification for erecting protective barriers, but rather, to become more aware and sensitive toward ourselves and others. God can take even the most painful of our experiences and work them out for our good and for His glory.

We openly declare ourselves to be His child. Let His healing power reign in wholeness!

♋

Sorting Us Out

By BETH & THE BUNCH

The form I show here is one way for everybody to know who is who in the System, what they are like, and who they know. This has been extremely helpful to me, as the host; to my therapists (I have three who work as a team); and to friends who know us.

As an alter "comes out," the helper in her house, either Amanda or Samantha, fills in the blanks about that alter. Sometimes that alter does not wish certain information to be included right away, so this chart is always changing. I try to keep on top of all the changes so that updates can be given to our therapists. This isn't always possible, because sometimes some alters don't want me to know if they have added anything.

But it helps me to know each alter and learn about them. It also helps because as the alters learn about each other and start talking to one another, they can add those names next to theirs. Sometimes it's like a mini-competition for the little ones, to see who knows the most.

I hope this will help other multiples learn their systems and open the communication lines.

My System							
Name	Age	Communicates With	Role	Feeling	Behavior	Likes	Dislikes
			Host				
Name	Age	Communicates With	Role	Feeling	Behavior	Likes	Dislikes

23rd Poetry

1. The inner parts are my family; I will try not to fear them.

2. Though a lot of them try to rob me of my senses.

3. Some lead me down misery lane because I ask for their name sake.

4. There are days I fear nothing because some of the inner family work with me.

5. Some of my inner family put their selves before me around a big mahogany table; We try to get to know each other, because there are times we feel that there are no others.

6. I pray that we can learn to live with each other, so that we may be able to work through hurt, sadness, hate, anger, shame...and love each other.

7. Then we can live with ourself forever.

Sincerely Yours, with Love

By Avon T.

♋

The First Time

By DIANNE D.

The fall is always a difficult time for me. Body memories and night terrors are painful and plentiful: my husband and two babies died in the Fall, and the creation of three of my most powerful alters occurred during the Fall and Winter months of my childhood. Just to make it to the New Year is a major achievement, so invariably I do not find myself out much during the Fall months, and when I am out, I am almost always terrified of everything. My family, my co-workers, my therapist, my friends all know Fall is the time when I am most likely to lose ground, not gain it. So this year, finding myself out more than in Falls past, I embarked on a strategy of changing the environment as much as I was able to, and expanding my support base to include people where I work.

Mind you, I didn't go in one day and decide I was going to tell my boss I am a multiple. No. I work for a man who is a no-nonsense, hardened war veteran who tolerates nothing outside of his own arena of blood-and-guts war stories, and who holds all studies of psychology in open contempt. What I did do was decide to attend an open support group held at the university where I work, for women who are survivors of sexual abuse. That in itself was a major step for me, because to do so was to finally admit the abuse and not leave any gray area in which I could comfortably deny it. Going was one thing; saying something as to why I was there, was quite another.

My heart beat so hard I was sure everyone in the room would see my dress leaping up and down over my left breast, and at times the sound of my own heartbeat was so loud in my ears, I could not hear the other women in the group clearly. Public speaking has always terrified me, and to reveal anything so terribly intimate to a cluster of strangers, was for me tantamount to walking across campus naked. There were a zillion other things I could think of that I would rather do than open my mouth and tell those fine women I was a multiple. Forty-five minutes into the hour-long session, I finally summoned all the courage I had and hesitantly told the two other women there not only was I a survivor of sexual abuse, but I am also a multiple, a direct result of the sexual and physical violence and emotional abandonment I experienced as a child.

Even as the words escaped my mouth, I felt an enormous weight being lifted from my shoulders. Whether or not the other women believed me was irrelevant; I had spoken the words to total strangers and they had not gotten up and fled the room in horror and neither had I dropped dead from the shock of saying it. I was positively euphoric! Contrary to what I had expected from the other women, I was received warmly and quietly, as if honoring my survival. There was no condemnation of the method I had chosen to survive, nor disbelief of my statement; I was accepted for who I was. Perhaps equally as surprising, the facilitator of the group did not banish me from attending. She was warm, accepting, and gave a mini-talk on the "defense mechanism" of multiplicity, so as to correct any misperceptions the other women might have privately had regarding MPD. The clincher came when the session ended and she invited everyone back the following week. I was no better and no worse than anyone else in the room, equally as deserving to be there; I had been welcomed into the group.

My weekly session with my therapist was to take place that evening and I couldn't wait to tell her! It was all I could do not to call her ahead of time. I knew she'd be aghast, because the Fall is so notoriously my worst time that she has long since given up trying to work on anything significant until the New Year. When the session finally arrived some four hours later, the news of my triumph comprised the first words out of my mouth. She was thrilled, she hugged me and said how proud she was of me, and it was that wonderful feeling of acceptance all over again. I had done (for me) the unthinkable, and I had not perished in the process — a point my therapist made sure I did not miss.

After my session was finished, I went to my friend's house and told her, and her response was to invite me out to dinner with her and her husband. This particular friend is an integrated multiple who is a therapist specializing in the treatment of multiples, so she has a *real* connection to how much it took for me to go to the group and say what I did. We laughed and giggled most of the evening away, and her ever-patient husband sat and listened as I rattled on about how scared I'd been and how it felt to tell a perfect stranger I was a multiple. It was a first step for me, in an effort to reverse the very survival technique I had created over thirty years ago.

Since the cardinal rule of multiplicity is hiding, it only made sense to me that in order to change my usual mode of response to stress and trauma (by hiding or having one of the others come out to handle it for me — another form of hiding), I'd need to change the very core of the mechanism. Scary as it was, I knew the core was me. I had to come out of hiding, a little at a time; I had to choose the time and place which was safest and most appropriate, and above all else, I had to do it in a way which was not injurious to any of my wonderful other people.

All these many years they have taken such wonderful care of me, protected me from things I would not have survived otherwise, and kept me alive when death would have made sense as a viable option, and so it was with tender regard for their feelings that I made my stand, ever-conscious of their fears of exposure, but confident I could take care of them now, if given the chance. All my life I had been the recipient of their unheard and largely unnoticed protection and care; now it was my turn to give back what I had been so lovingly given for three-fourths of my life. The irony of my triumph is I know I would not have been able to do what I did without their help, without their cooperation, so I am still the recipient of their love and protection even as I sought to love and protect them. It was the first time I had ever said to them, "I will take care of *you*, I will not let any harm come to *you*, I will protect *you*." I had made their feelings my priority, and in doing so, I had validated them as the group had validated me. I gave them my acceptance, and in doing so, I had learned what it felt like to be accepted.

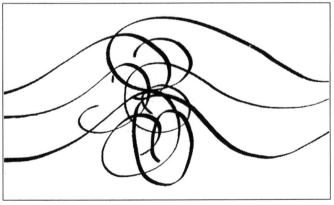

Inner Dynamics
By Sue K.

Organizing for Health

By ELEXIS

I have learned not to put anything down, outside.

I used to go to the store and put my keys or my hat on the counter while I opened my wallet. It seems as if I left my keys over a thousand times, and sometimes didn't remember which store I left them in.

Now, I place things in my pocket or in my backpack. I know, if I put it down, I've lost it.

I have learned to *write* things down if I'm supposed to remember them. No matter how hard I try, no matter how confident I feel, I always "forget." So — I write it down.

I've learned to keep "one" of everything. In the past I'd have six or seven calendars because I'd always lose one or two. But everything just got more confused. I had six or seven keychains, six or seven bags, etc. I started to get rid of all the excess baggage, and now with one calendar, one notebook, and one bag, it's much easier to know what I'm doing. And if I lose it, I just look for it. It's always *somewhere* in my house.

I've learned to stop trying to please everyone. That usually just splits me up more. I try to make my more "sensible" me happy and explain to others that it's just got to be that way.

I've asked myself *Who do I want to be?*

and I got the answer —

I want to be me...just *me*.

A responsible, caring individual who will make a difference in this world.

And that's just who I'll be —

By sharing with you —

The things that help me!

♋

Two Contracts

By STEPHANIE

Official Pardon

This Document is to hereby officially grant Unconditional Pardon to _____ as an act designed to free the aforementioned subject by the Jury, the Head of which shall be herein referred to as the Translator, guided and instructed by His Honor, Pegasus the Guardian.

A Pardon is granted that _____ may from hereon until eternity be granted access to all memories and feelings from any other part therein. The Jury recognizes a Pardon denotes innocence from conception, that any deed having been carried out whether in thought, word or action was done solely for the Watcher's safety of mind and body, regardless of the consequences thereafter, which have no bearing on this Official Pardon. The original motive for the supposed crime was Love, and Love cannot, in all fairness and logic, be judged.

Regret for incarceration is heartfelt and the hand of justice may reach out too late for some, but it is the sincere wish of the Jury, headed by the Watcher, that the part in pardon will reach out and accept the offer of restitution.

Restitution consists of a place within the system without shackles and constant overriding. Freedom to speak and to listen. To be heard and taken seriously.

Welcome Back!

♋

Safety Contract

I, Steph for Everyone, being one, many in one, or one of many, hereby enter into a safety contract between myself and the rest of the parts of me, or myself and my therapist, counselor or teacher, all terms being interchangeable.

For clarity, the questions such as WHY, HOW, and WHAT will be set forth, the answers coming from knowledge already assimilated but possibly forgotten.

By entering this contract, I express my willingness to learn and become aware of what I do to harm myself and why I do it. These are the hardest truths to look in the eye but it is necessary for healing. The original reason for self-destruction is Protection, but once this truth is realized, I can change the harmful behavior to one that is nurturing and helpful to the healing of Mind, Spirit and Body.

Before Self-Harm is defined, it is necessary to understand why a safety contract is mandatory to the healing process.

1) Trust, for many people, has been broken in the past, and while it becomes automatic not to trust others, it is easiest not to trust oneself. Therefore, a safety contract fosters trust between Oneself and Oneself, or between Oneself and any Other who is chosen to participate in this agreement.

2) Though sometimes I can be clear as to what is happening in my life, often it is one big storm and I lose sight of who I am and what I am doing. A safety contract can provide tangible proof that I am working hard and have a clear sense of purpose. It may also provide a lifeline when I am in danger of hurting myself and don't have the apparent strength to know what to do next.

A definition of what safety *is* can also be defined by what self-harm entails. The following is a partial list, for only I myself know how I define self-harm, and any of the following can be modified, deleted, or added to at any time:

1) Chemical abuse.

2) Alcohol.

3) Any sharp object.

4) Any blunt instrument.

5) Any binding tool, e.g., rope, handcuffs, etc.

6) Any reckless behavior that puts me in danger, even something as innocent as driving, or a sport that is potentially dangerous if I don't follow safety rules.

7) Resistance to therapeutic suggestions.

8) Refusing to learn alternative methods of coping. This is *not* the same as not *knowing* alternate methods of coping.

9. Knowingly placing myself in victimization roles or retraumatization. Please note the use of the word *"knowingly."* It is very important.

Just as there are many reasons for signing a Safety Contract, I know I can think of reasons for *not* signing, but I acknowledge that these reasons are *not* willfulness, or born of a desire to hurt myself. They are the result of a lifetime of pain, suffering, and coping with the unmanageable, and are therefore quite natural. However, once recognized, they can be analyzed and defused, ultimately replaced with joy and acceptance of myself and pride in my accomplishments.

These reasons are possible, and not necessarily everyone's experience. Again, they can be modified, deleted or added to at any time for the purpose of self-exploration and healing.

1) Pressure: By others who don't understand the process of my healing journal.

By my inner parts who are resisting communication.

2) Fear: Of joy. Often happiness has been only conditional and therefore not to be trusted. This contract can lead to joy, and therefore, experience tells us, is not to be trusted. We can learn that we *can* trust. This contract will help.

3) Experience: Pain often seems a way of validating our existence and is something I can control, or believe I can control. Therefore, pain is familiar, and it is always hard to give up the familiar. But if we know we can replace pain with behavior that feels good and is healing, it will be easier to give up that which is harmful.

This contract may seem lengthy, but it needs to be clear and defined. This contract is in no way a statement of how things *have to be*. It is written by human hand, not Divine Inspiration, and can be modified by any person to meet their needs.

This contract is signed by Stephanie & the Cast, and _____ on the date of _____. Following are phone numbers for support and need:

Friend_____

Friend_____

Therapist_____

Hospital_____

(Signed by Pax, Pegasus, Jessie, Twins, Camille, Jessica, C.K., Jenny & Sparrow & others.)

♋

A Multiple Of Rights

1. Each self has the right to exist and be recognized.
2. Each self has the right to be listened to by the others.
3. Each self has the right to feel any emotion.
4. Each self has the right to express feelings.
5. Each self has the right to time "out."
6. Each self has the right to disagree with the others or anyone else.
7. Each self has the right to be happy.
8. Each self has the right to have needs and wants respected.
9. Each self has the right to have needs met.
10. Each self has the right to make mistakes.
11. Each self has the right to have a voice in decisions.
12. Each self has the right to be loved.
13. Each child self has the right to be childish.
14. No self has a right to harm any other.

Mostly by Melanie, Duncan, Casey and L.H., but everybody had input. We are working on a list of responsibilities.

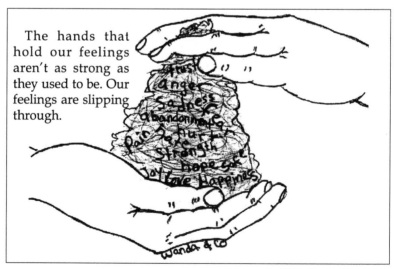

The hands that hold our feelings aren't as strong as they used to be. Our feelings are slipping through.

By Wanda & Co.

Touching

By RACHEL

If therapists agree to hold alters, how do you learn to hold and embrace them yourself? How do other people with MPD not get torn up when their therapists touch them? I have alters who want Rick to touch them or hold them, but there are other parts (I don't like the word *alter*) who would never trust him or talk to him, or who would give control to him in unhealthy ways, and I never would have learned how to hold them and love them myself. Am I the only MPD person who feels that way?

It seems as if lots of people who have MPD write about their therapists holding and touching younger alters, and they usually write about it as a positive — it wouldn't be, for us.

Doesn't that also prevent parts from feeling the pain of not being touched and held in healthy ways when they were little? I know the grief Laurie went thru with those feelings, and it helped her grow by feeling that. It helped her learn to nurture and care for herself.

It was talking about what Laurie wanted and didn't get that made her feel the pain that motivated her to take care of herself, and me to find a way to hold her.

I think therapists who agree to hold younger alters aren't helping people with MPD to grow. Maybe therapists who do that can't really hear or witness the pain of younger parts.

Mending

A person has three parts: Body, Soul, and Spirit. To be whole, to be mended, you have to strike a balance within these three parts.

The soul tormented by memory must be tenderly cradled while the body and spirit fight for balance, for wholeness, allowing God to touch here and there until we are mended into ourselves.

By Paul in Stacy Joy

♋

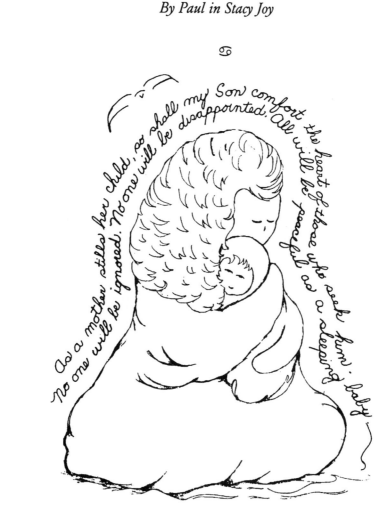

Comforting
By Beth Gassen-Parsons

ABC Therapy

By Linda L. McNulty

ABC therapy is as simple as 1,2,3. What better way to tap into your childhood than to use a very familiar childhood activity. Recently I found myself wanting to write the ABC's, as an adult. I thought this to be very childish, but then again I have not been able to get in touch with my childhood. My inner child does not speak but, I realized that she had a lot to say. I found that the ABC writing was an appeal by the inner child to talk. I then wrote down the ABC's and used free association (the first word that came to mind).

I requested information from birth to age 19. I found that I could access many events in a way that did not bring about fear or the sense that I was telling family secrets. I had never been able to remember what age these events happened. All I knew was that somehow I became an adult.

But through the ABC's I remembered being age 6; I remembered things that I was afraid of and lots of other information.

I took this approach two steps further. If it worked for me, perhaps it would work for siblings and parents, if they were agreeable to such an assignment. My brother (the youngest sibling) as well as my mother and father, agreed. Each used free association pertaining to their birth to age 19.

This really opened the door. I was able to see the pattern of behavior and thought processes that had been passed on from generation to generation. Several letters of the alphabet were labeled, in some instances, identically to one or more of those participating. I obtained information to the origin of some of my thoughts, not to mention a lot of answers to my parents' behavior.

So this has proved quite therapeutic to me. I was able to take these answers with me and later take a closer look that accessed more of my stifled childhood. We (myself, brother and parents) did share our answers with each other, and often laughed. This made talking to each other comfortable. As we shared our answers we elaborated on each to gain an understanding of where the response came from.

ABC therapy can also be used with an internal system/family, where different parts, sides, ego states, etc. have difficulty expressing.

This allowed those parts to be known as a valued part of the system and a means to communicate in a non-threatening manner.

For an example of how it works, on a piece of paper write down the ABC's using a line for each letter, then ask those participating to write through free association, the first thing that comes to mind, next to the letter, bearing in mind that it is the choice of the participants to share some or not at all. If you can't label each letter it is OK. I often put out a dictionary for those who need a little help. Then after ample time to do the ABC's, I ask each participant to share the answers with each other, once again by choice.

The topic you want to use ABC therapy with is up to you. For example, using an internal system, I would say:

My dear internal system,

This is Linda. I am stuck at this point in my recovery, and I know how important you are to me, and the valuable information that you hold. I am asking if you would help me by doing an activity with me. I am particularly interested in how you can help me stay safe. It is not mandatory, and I respect your decision to participate or not, as well as value your opinion.

Respectfully yours,
Linda

I waited, and this is what happened:

Response from internal system

I would love to help. Thank you for asking. - June.

A. Alone (do not set yourself up by being alone)

B. Busy (stay busy)

C. Call (set up with someone you can call or stay with if feeling unsafe)

D. Distance (keep a distance from unsafe things)

E. Eyes open (look all around you)

Etc.

Response from another internal member

I can't help on this one, but thanks for including me. - D.D.

Sure, I can give some suggestions. - Julian

A. Access (access all those who can help from inside and outside. Make a directory.)

B. Buy (You know this one works. Go shopping.)

C. Castle (Your safe internal space, with a security system. Make a room reservation.)

D. Direct (Designate a chief of security from the internal system)

Etc.

So there you have it: an easy, spontaneous way to communicate, access, gain insight, or whatever your need is. I hope this can be as valuable to others in their journey of self-discovery and recovery as it has been for me.

♋

Looking Out
By Sue K.

Story Therapy

By SARAI (L.M.)

In the age of individual therapy, group therapy, movement therapy, art therapy, occupational therapy etc., can there be room for another therapeutic modality as simple as story therapy? For many of us who deal with painful childhood memories as an adult, one more modality is one more way of doing memory work. I have found that story therapy allows my memories to become more manageable. Story therapy allows me to place the memory in front of me, whether it is a story from my own creative subconscious or from another source. Through this I am able to reach a point of personalizing that story and finding the parallel it holds within me.

Stories that I have written, such as *Dreuyfus the Dragon, The Apple Tree That Would Not Let Go Of Its Apples,* and *Frieda The Goodnight Fairy* often have no immediate meaning to me. Later I see the significance, or friends or family see a parallel that I often cannot see. It is also easier for significant others to deal with a story and perhaps shed further light on the memory as it has or had affected them in their own personal way.

As an adult it is helpful to deal with childhood memories with a story, or on a teddy-bear security level, to judge our behavior at the level in which it happened. The adult who remembers the behavior of an inner seven-year- old (for example) is often critical and unforgiving, creating a situation which may lead to destructive behavior.

So the stories that I share started out in the bedroom of a five -year-old, spontaneous and unpremeditated. As the stories were told and told and refined, I soon saw that they were stories of my life, my childhood, my painful experiences, but they now became something manageable, something inside of me brought *outside* that I could hear, touch, and feel.

As the stories became known, I was asked to share them in a group therapy session with people recovering from similar events. Their responses were touching, and allowed them to personalize the story and bring out something from within themselves, in a non-threatening way.

How often have we said or heard, "I have a friend who has this problem...what do you think she/he should do?" And often it is ourselves who have the problem.

When we put the problem in the context of another we are given permission to share and relieve some anxiety in a manageable way. So story therapy is yet another way to work with painful memories or bring them to the surface gently. Whatever way you use stories, look to your childhood not only for memories, but for ways to manage them.

♋

Group Therapy
By Julie - The Learner

Deb's Idea

By DEBORAH

Hello! My name is Deborah Jane. I am now integrated, and one of my biggest fears was to feel my own feelings.

Pain and fear are the most difficult to handle. So what I do for myself is, I get really comfortable and then I allow myself to feel my pain (or fear, or anger — whatever feeling I may be working with) fully. Then I get in touch with whoever else inside may be sharing the feeling — like my child self, or my teen self, or maybe an alter. I ask them if they would like to help me deal with this feeling. If they do, I imagine that we are very small — about two inches high — and we go inside my body and sit down on chairs before the feeling.

Once when I was working with the pain, I invited my 15-year-old self to sit with me. We looked at the pain. It was much bigger than we were. It was radiating. It had tar and nicotine all over it and was covered with about five inches of volcanic ash.

I asked my teenager if she wanted to help me blow the ash off. She did, so we stood up and blew it off together. Then we decided to massage our pain. It made us feel better — and we weren't afraid of our pain anymore!

We talked to our pain, and assured it that as long as we are alive, we will always be there to support our pain and nurture it. (Thus we are supporting and nurturing ourselves!)

My teen and I held hands together and smiled. Together, we could embrace our pain. We were glad we could actively do something to overcome our fear of feeling.

You can do this with any feeling! I hope it helps others.

♋

It's OK To Be ME

It's OK to be ME
Regardless of where I may be.

It's OK to be ME
Sad and miserable as I can be.

It's OK to be ME
Happy and glad, completely carefree.

It's OK to be ME
When I am as angry as I wish to be.

It's OK to be ME
When I am somewhere in between.

It's OK to be ME
When I can't even be seen.

It's OK to be ME
When I am afraid, lost and alone.

It's OK to be ME
This mind, body, and spirit, you see, is my true home.

In my home I am entitled to feel free
To accept or reject that which I see.

The choice cannot be made for me.
It is mine to make, and mine alone.

One day soon I'll find a way to make
Self-like, Self-love, Self-respect, Self-Confidence
Self-trust and Self-esteem my very own.

By Melody Sue McCurry

♋

Physical Healing

How do so many people start to be physically healthy after life-times of neglect?

By D. and ASSOCIATES

I asked one day
What would we need
To Be
Physically Healthy and Strong?
Voices answered me —
to my surprise —
   in an overwhelming sadness:
"To be clean"
Some said
"To walk"
Some said
"To rest"
Some said
"To eat right"
Some said
"To quit smoking"
Some said
"To help Others"
Some said
But how?
I wondered and pondered
the thoughts
I heard
And suddenly began
to cry
"I don't know how"
I said...
"Bathe the Little Ones first,
Then gently put them
to bed,
Then take your bath"
Our therapist suggested.
"Measure the bath water

with a thermometer,"
She said.
We have a candy thermometer
in the kitchen!
"Find a special shower Inside
where the clean air comes in
and the dirty feelings come out
through the pores in The Body's
skin.
The special colored water
Will wash all those dirty
feelings away down the drain,"
She continued.
"Then a bath can be something
you do just to smell nice."

I cried.
Will this work?
We want it so.
Spirit Friend, please be our Guide.
Hope, please be our strength.
Faith, please be our courage.
Other Protectors, can you lead the way?
We want to be physically healthy.
Little Bit says
Starting at the top of
a list is a
Beginning.
We are Beginning.
We will wash away
the Guilt and Shame —
put the blame where
it belongs —
Back to our abusers
Not inside of us
We deserve to be
Physically healthy and
Strong.
Even though all the
answers aren't found,
That doesn't mean there
are none.

United We Stand
Looking forward
Not back
This is a new Day
We are Survivors
We are Holding On
We will believe
We will try
We will cry
And One Day
We will look back and
Smile.
Because we will be
Physically Healthy.
There is
Joy in the Journey.
Good luck to all of you
Who share in similar Struggles
We hope you too will
Succeed.
We hope this
Helps...
For All of Us.

♋

Waiting for Something Wonderful

By DOTTIE

I never did exactly understand integration. I just knew it was a goal of therapy and that when it came it would be important. And wonderful. So I kept working at therapy and waiting for it to come. And waiting for it to come. And waiting for it to come.

While I was waiting I started looking around at some of the young women at my work. They were enjoying relationships with the men in their lives. They weren't scared, or crying, or embarrassed. They weren't flying out of the room or counting to endure. They weren't stiff, lifeless lumps. They were happy.

I began to be angry that I couldn't have what other women had. One therapist told me to send my little ones off to play in another room. Guess I only have little ones, because when I sent mine off to play there was no one left with my husband but the lifeless body he was accustomed to. We were being cheated out of an important part of an adult relationship because some selfish pig abused a child he should have cared for and protected. I looked at those other women and I got even angrier. I continued therapy and I waited, but nothing wonderful was happening.

So I tried a different tactic. I told my little ones they should stay in the room, that he wasn't going to hurt them, that they should give him a chance, but I promised that the instant they felt they were being hurt they could go. Then I reassured them over and over that everything was OK, that nothing hurt, that he wasn't that person they were afraid of. At first they could hardly stay any time at all. They had to fly away and I couldn't stop them. But little by little they have learned that it is OK to stay.

I'm still not sure what integration is. But I am not waiting for it to happen anymore. Life is a whole lot happier when everyone stays in the same body, in the same room, at the same time, in the same life. Maybe that is enough. Or maybe that *is* integration.

Work Together or Shut Up

By STACY JOY

Inner communication is probably one of the most important skills for anyone like us, with MPD.

We started out scattered and unwilling to talk to anyone other than the person who did the most journaling. It overwhelmed her. Then one day a strong male voice spoke up and started his own dictatorship. It was *work together or shut up*. He saw the exhaustion "she" was going through, so he came along to bully us into place.

He (Mr. C.), the journaling woman (Martha), and David, began to sort things out. Mr. C. and David worked hard to first force us,then teach us that we all have to work together or someone would kill the rest in suicide.

In the beginning it was very hard. But the three of them gave us no choice. Everything went into the journal and therapy.

That was three-and-a-half years ago. Little by little we began to communicate...insults, threats etc., included. But it was a start. The more we worked together, the less domineering Mr. C. became. He and his partner are usually still the leaders, but through Godly compassion, not brute strength. He set up the rules: no sex, drugs, alcohol, cutting, burning, suicide...and to work with our treatment team at all times.

Now we group up interchangeably, and get on with life. But the key to unlock the prison doors we lived behind was to communicate and work together.

We now have networks, working groups, single specialists, and our own personal army. (We were in the Air Force for a while.)

This communication has kept us alive, given us hope, and has brought us from being suicidal every day to the understanding that suicide is stupid.

We have too much to live for, and we didn't have to integrate to get this far. We still have a long road, but together we can do it. And some of these guys in here really are fun to talk to and joke with. Some of the stuff that gets said (and when it gets said) is so funny it's hard not to burst out laughing on the bus or in church, etc.

But of course there's the serious side. With internal communication, you can always find a companion to lean on, who is willing to share the load of hurt or anger, the emotions that come with daily life. We leave each other notes: "Do this on this date," etc. So if there is a blackout, the important things get done.

But with our communication now, the blackouts aren't so often or so bad, since more than one person has the necessary information.

It's certainly something to think about. Working together is much more healthy than suicide. Just remember...it's hard at first, but then becomes fun.

Realizing we are One
By Paula

Release Pain

Return to childhood
Endure the memories
Let go of the pain.
Every day it eases
And lifts the weight of sorrow.
Shame and guilt slip away
Ending the trauma.

Put to rest the rage
And begin to know yourself.
It is a tragedy of the past;
Now, experiment with life.

By Paula Hurwitz

♋

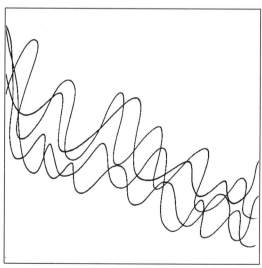

Braided Forms II
By Sue K.

Employment & Dissociative Disorder

By DILLY AND THE PROTECTORS

Keeping a job is a balancing act; I (we) think being MPD makes it possible.

I work in a very closed field. There is no branching off to another area or field of work. Many is the day I (we) must juggle what is going on in the real world and what's going on in my head.

To be real honest, our job has kept us alive. There are days if we would not have had a job to go to we would have died at home. The job has kept us centered and kept us from going inside ourselves permanently.

Don't get me wrong; it's not been easy keeping this job. There have been many days I've wanted to quit and run. I have had to teach others in my system parts of my job and the children have had to learn to let me alone at work. In turn I give them special time at home. Some days that's easier said than done, but somehow we all get through the work day.

Over a year ago I was hospitalized. I was forced to tell my boss about my disorder. It was devastating. He knew nothing about MPD; he was scared. Before I went to the hospital I had to sign papers in which my job was at stake. I was angry and scared all at the same time. But in the long run, I was lucky. My boss took an interest in MPD and was willing to learn a little about it. One year later the papers I signed have been torn up. I believe my boss trusts me to do my job to the best of my ability (which sometimes means "our abilities.") I'm glad I could keep my job.

My therapy and my job can make for some very hard days at work. But hard work can also keep me from self-destructing. It helps me concentrate on the here and now.

Nowadays if I have a hard therapy session, I'm brave enough to tell my boss. Somehow doing this has helped me to not screw up. I guess it takes pressure off me to be my best, and in turn I end up doing OK. Having a job also keeps me in contact with non-MPD people which helps me see there is something to being integrated someday.

A job may not be for everyone, but for me (us) it pays for my therapy and keeps me going.

♋

Team Work

By KATHY with US backing up

For us, to continue working has been one of the more demanding aspects of this process.

We started at our current job two and a half years ago, taking on a new challenge in our career. The job consists of heavy phone sales selling research services to marketing and sales professionals, as well as contact with clients and going out and meeting strangers to sell the market research services. We make approximately 50 or 60 phone calls a day to clients and prospective clients. Our job is flexible. Right now, we work Monday, Wednesday and Friday, and go to therapy on Tuesday and Thursdays.

The multiplicity first came up a little over a year ago, and we went to work completely flipped out for eight months. We would leave at lunch time and I would drive my car and have lunch in my car and just flip out. I would sit and shake in terror. People would come out and write in our journal. It was just a part of the "I am learning I am one of a system and my ego is completely overwhelmed about it" times. Then I would drive back to work and sit and work.

Learning about boundaries has been hard: both internal boundaries and setting limits with the little ones. The little ones started therapy first and it took some time for my older ones to come forward to help (in part due to my attitude) . So it was basically me and the little ones. The day would drag endlessly; time passed so slowly. It was extremely difficult. All day I would sit at the computer and be completely wigged out and still I was able to get through the day. It has settled down a lot after realizing the system was not out to get me, we just needed to work on *who* is out in the body *when*. I also needed to adjust myself to accepting help from the inside and not doing it "alone." It has helped to have different people assigned to different jobs so they can be part of the work. They feel satisfaction and enjoyment with the rewards that come from being employed (like expressing our creativity and business skills, having money for stuffed animals, toys, ice cream, clothes—not to mention our safe home space, building "selves" esteem and keeping our feet in the present) .

This second year has been slightly easier. There have been several personalities — Charlie, Joey, Trish and Shoshannah — who have helped quite a bit. Charlie blocks the pain a lot, so he takes over when the pain is too much to bear. He can just ignore it completely and do the job. Over time, though, he has gotten very good at interacting with strangers, and he is tough. He asks for the sales order much more bluntly and effectively than is my style.

There have been two scares—two times where I was certain we were going to lose control. One time we (the system) were going to meet a sales prospect. We got to his office and it turned out that a consultant from another company was going to sit in on the meeting. We got completely triggered and almost lost our composure. Little Trish, who is three, was begging to come out to crawl under the table because she was so scared. My urge was to sit my 32-year-old body down on the floor in my suit and crawl underneath the feet of these two gentlemen, and ask them to call our therapist, Amy. At that time, the inner voices were very much closer to me all the time, and I could hear the battle on the inside even as my hand was reaching out to shake theirs and we exchanged business cards.

No, Trish, you can't do that. They will call the men in white coats to come get us; they don't know about little people in big people's bodies.

Somebody from inside came forward and got her to move back, as I began fumbling my way through the sales presentation. It was really bad; I felt like I was coming unglued by the minute and found myself bargaining with God. It turned out that I got the sale on the spot. The prospect said, "Great, sign me up. We will try your service for a year." It was a very good lesson in how intense the inner experience can be, and how it does not show as much as we think it does on the outside.

I don't think it will happen that way again. People on the inside know much better what to look out for. Sometimes triggers for us happen when there are surprises and the right people on the inside aren't in the right places. Trish now does not go to meetings, she just gets to put the stamps and stickers on the envelopes at the end of the day. Three-year-olds generally cannot be articulate or excel in conversations about high technology markets, or discuss when the market is going to turn up, etc...

The second hard time regarding work happened when my boss and I went together to a meeting and he informed us ten minutes prior to departure that we were going to do the presentation. Now it had never been that way before; normally either I go, or we go together and he presents. People on the inside were experiencing tremendous internal confusion as we tried to get the materials ready. Everyone was talking at once, resulting in a muddle of loud confusion. We got there and took a deep breath and we managed fine.

Shoshannah, a fourteen-year-old in the system, came forward and asked the children to please step back much farther inside, that there was nothing they could do to help, and that Kathy and Charlie were going to take care of it. A couple little ones were not moving fast enough so I said on the inside *If you go inside further, later on we can go get ice cream.* Calmness ensued and the meeting went fine.

It was a real marker, being one of the first times that I, Kathy, felt a sense of trust towards the system. Often before, I felt as if they were trying to do me in, when actually everyone was simply having big emotions at times that were not convenient for me.

We have learned a lot about working and doing our healing process at the same time. It is very, very hard, but for us working is good because it has helped us maintain some semblance of structure in the life we share. On the other hand, we do not want to misrepresent ourselves. For the first year, in dealing with the sheer volume of presenting personalities, feelings, memories, every workday was an immense challenge to get through. In the bigger picture, work has given us all a sense of accomplishment and has been one of the best ways to learn cooperating and communicating.

This past month, we've had the hardest time dealing with new memories, intense feeling states and losing more time than usual. The outer reality was that during this same period, we had a record sales month. Even more ironic: some of our best sales days followed terrible days of crying, shaking, and having intense feelings...as if the two had nothing to do with each other. Odd world we live in.

We are not trying to make light of multiplicity or dealing with the abuse. But sometimes I do have to laugh. I have to laugh when work gets done in mysterious ways. I have to laugh when Joey, an eight-year-old, says *I have a great idea for a new marketing campaign,* and we implement her ideas, and sales increase 30%. For us, it is selves-empowering and selves- esteeming.

It has been an amazing discovery to realize through work that all the energy we use to hide our multiplicity can also be used to direct our collective creativity in ways that build our selves-esteem.

THE KIDS' PERSPECTIVE

It goes better because we feel safer now. It goes better because we get other time to be out at home besides work time. It goes better because we have jobs at work and get to help. It goes better because we all feel better when it goes good and not so hard all the time. Learning takes time for us. For so long no one heard or seen us. If we didn't work, no structure would mean big feelings all the time, big hardness always. We need structure and cookies and ice cream and regular life just like other people.

Written by us younger ones who are big helpers now.

♋

God helps me protect the Kids inside.
By Wanda & Co.

Creative Coping

By STACY JOY

Avoiding self-destructive tendencies involves learning special survival skills and how to apply them in times of danger.

First, try to keep the tools used for hurting out of the house, or have a hiding spot to put them in...a spot that is off-limits to everyone except the Protectors. I have two places: a box on the top shelf that's inconvenient to reach, or in the trunk. If it's in the trunk (which I use as a counter) , I have to move the microwave. The Protectors notice.

We also have a lock to put on it, with the key placed where it is difficult to get. That takes time and signals a Red Alert.

A Red Alert sends a safety plan into action...either your own plan or back-up help from a treatment team.

An example of a personal plan: when my "kids" want to hurt the body we get them candy and bubble gum, if we can. We try to keep some in the house. Toys, books, etc. can be used as diversions. For the upper ages, art is a very important tool. Get the person to sketch the pain and need, to externalize the need. The sketches might hurt the eyes and hearts, but they leave the life and skin intact.

We have a "bad" bear. The person who gave it to us hurt us very badly with false accusations and lies about us. We never liked this bear. We took it so we wouldn't hurt her feelings. So when we are angry, we pound it around. When my son was here, he used it too for his anger. The first thing he did was pull its eyes off. I know most bears are to love and comfort with, but this is Bad Bear, who we can punch or kick. A Bop Clown would do the same thing: punch it and it comes back to punch again.

Self-destructive tendencies are internalized pain and anger, so you need to externalize these feelings. Write an angry poem, rip newspapers into tiny bits, put the anger and pain out, not in. My phone book can fly! (Ha Ha!)

Just today, we had to use our kid skills. A four-year-old is very violent and angry. For two days, someone wants to burn. We are mad at our psychiatrist right now, so we wrote a letter using appropriate language and attitudes to tell him why. We may send it after our therapist sees it.

We try to be responsible, always looking for new ways to fight the need to hurt the body. We have been very successful, considering the stress of the last couple months. We visited our daughter on a psych ward yesterday. She had hurt her hand on purpose. It hurt me to see my child doing the things I had done. But she never saw our burns or cuts.

The pain has to stop, and it has to stop within ourselves...one personality helping another to get past the desire to hurt, and learn to help protect the flesh and life.

♋

Hope rising out of darkness.
By Linda G.

When one of us is in crisis, we surround them in a soft pink bubble and let them float away until we are safe again in therapy. This keeps the rest of us functioning. Thanks, Deena, for this gift.

By Wanda

Chapter

3

Fighting the Good Fight

Persistence in the face of pain

Rages

I earned my name. I held all the anger for many years.

Now I give it back bit by bit so they, my friends inside, may process in therapy. My comment or lesson:

Rage can do two things: keep you sick, or be used to fight your way out. If I come against a tough spot I use my anger to say
NO.

I can and will do this.

I've been put down enough.

By Rages in Stacy Joy

♋

My Alpha Female
By Steph & the Cast

Digging Up

I've spent so many years
digging my being into this hole
that it seems impossible
to set myself in reverse
in order to scramble back out.
Yet, climb out I must
or forever remain in the darkness
of self-illusion and its infringing despair.
Inevitably we're all left with ourselves,
but better to have remaining a self in honesty
than one clothed in the deceit of unacknowledgment.
For what benefit to deny
the perceptions of our identity,
to mask from ourselves what we are
when everything else
that touches upon us
falls away with the nature of time.
Even knowing this,
I always furtively attempt
to hold onto these external particulars,
thinking that somehow they will
lead me to contentment.
But in the end
they possess no magical power
to soothe the sensitivities and hurts
of thirty-some odd years —
the accumulation is beyond
their scope of remedy
and I'm called once again
to rely on my own self-worth,
which is still at the end of this poem
struggling to surmount
the edge of the hole
it dug for itself.

By Pseudo

We in Violent Peaceful Life

Evil Baby guards us in a Fonzie-like style
    replete with leather jacket and sub-machine guns.
Michael cries out warnings and bangs
    on the war drums.
The Sargeant leads the fighting ones into
    battle so we'll survive.
Genevieve reminds us to enjoy smiling face
    mustard-mouthed fish in the river.
Jennifer cuts up women dolls and
    smears everything with killer worm blood.
Mommy Sally spanks us and tells us
    stories and holds us.
Teacher Sally shows us different ways
    to try and work together.
Healthy Sally brings up ideas on varied
    ways to view things.
Healer Sally hypnotizes us often and
    regresses us to babyhood.
Kieyeser and Jeffrey are violent kids
    enjoying violent play.
Recorder/Reporter often writes and speaks
    for all of us each day.
Little Sally is a unit. All members by
    this name.
We don't all know each other and
    some hate others but we are not the same.
We are the world in one body, society
    in one flesh.
We can teach the world how
    to blend, how better to mesh.
We encourage creation of places
    for violent ones.
And unconditional love and
    acceptance-and-joy of them/us.
Why do you make us go to jail
    or war to express ourselves?
Now you ban our books, art and
    even music.
You give us ultimatums: change,
    die, or be imprisoned.

No voice, no rights, no dignity,
   no personhood.
When all non-violent options for
   violent expression are denied,
only violence is left, so it's
   be violent or die.

We could have our own island or state.
Having fighting games, be employed to
   engage in fist-fighting debates.
We could write stories and movies,
   songs and plays,
Yet you say we can't exist as us
   and want us put away.
We could demolish old buildings,
   build dams preventing floods.
Send us to dig graves,
   knock down walls and drive trucks.
Don't make us co-exist with women
   who refuse to provide for us.
We first were hurt by women who
   abused and neglected us.
And by men who failed to protect
   us from their neglect and abuse.
Our hatred for women was and
   is caused by women.
So let us live in peaceful
   violence — just being ourselves.
To be a hating violent peaceful
   force for healing and for love.
Give us a place where we may
   fight, destroy and kill
animals for food, and items that
   must be destroyed anyway.
We won't bother you if you don't
   bother us.
But we'll share our food and our
   world — 'cause we are part of *us*.

By Sally B.

Nights

My hands are shaking in dread
    Of the movies rewinding yet again
Preparing for their next showing
    An eternity in slow motion

My eyes are stinging from lack of sleep
    My head is carrying its weight of remembered dread
I cannot help but wonder
    Will it ever end
This multitude within me
    Crying for recognition

Perhaps if I remain awake a moment longer
    My eyes will open and truly see
The horrors my children are living
    Scattering now...these seeds of a dandelion

What effort I am making to bring them home...
    None but me will ever know.

By Dorene

♋

A Symbolic Act

Thrusts of anger into the faceless body
　　clear the soul of oppressive rage.
The knife's downward path hits its mark
　　again and again and again.

It is only a survivor's drawing on paper
　　but it is the face of a prior reality.
Freeing the brain of fury and wrath —
　　the rampaging storm subsides into grief.

Sobbing sounds and screams fill the air
　　as untold years of emotions are released.
I am alive and I am powerful!
　　Killing him in absentia gives me strength.

By Paula Hurwitz

♋

Multiple Crossing
By Libby

Win

So now I worry
wait
worry some more
pace
try to be normal
no bad thoughts
do the right things
wait
hope
breathe
I want out
no fuss
no yell
no banging on the wall
this is a test
don't screw up
you want to go home
you are better
you can make it
this time is different
you have enough scars
enough tears
enough hate
breathe
in the nose
out of the mouth
but the anger is in me
enough to push
talk, scream
I'm so proud
I know I can make it
I'm going to win.

By Jami Daun

♋

Living Well

Living isn't easy but you've got to begin
The past haunts you but you can start again
You can feel the fire but you can't touch the flame
You can't drown in the pool around you
But you can stand in the rain
You can cut jokes but you can't break the skin
Living well may hurt but it's sure not a sin
And I want to, Yes I want to — Oh yeah
I want to...

By Chew of KGP

♋

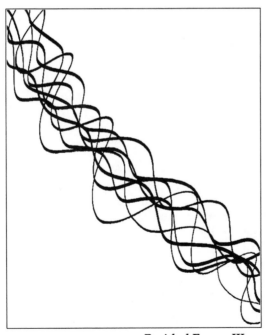

Braided Forms III
By Sue K.

Demons From Two Points of View

I.

Ghosts of the past hover over my bed.
There's no rest for the wicked, Somebody said.
No! She's not wicked, she's a scared, lonely child
Who longs for a night when the demons aren't wild.

To dream of wild horses and angels with wings,
A mommy who loves her & holds her & sings.
I plead for my child, *Keep the demons away.*
Please! No more screams in the darkness, I pray.

But we can't find the God who watches the night.
The bed isn't safe. The child wakes in fright.
We can't fight the terror alone in our bed.
But one day we'll win. The demons will be dead.

Now we sleep on the floor & the demons don't see
That the bed is now empty. At last we are free.
My child falls asleep, a bear under her arm.
The angels and I will keep her from harm.

II.

To hell with you, demons!
You're stealing our life.
We're so tired of running.
We've decided to fight.

You've taken so much
There's been too many tears.
Now we've run from our bed
Consumed by the fears.

You can't have our bed!
We won't hide anymore.
What else can you take?
We're sick of this war.

We deserve our warm bed.
We deserve to feel safe.
To hell with you, demons!

We scream in your face.

This pain of the past,
We can use it to fight
It took incredible strength
Now we're seeking the light.

I'm a survivor!
Believe it or not.
I knew fear, I knew pain,
I cried but I FOUGHT!

Now my life is my own.
The abusers are gone,
But you demons took over
And I am your pawn.

TO HELL WITH YOU, DEMONS!
You won't win this fight.
I am strong! I am tough!
You will not take my life!

By Janne

♋

The Journey

It is a long journey
towards healing
Sometimes it feels like I have come
so far
Other times
like today
it feels like there is so far to go
the trip endless
    exhausting
the goal
    unreachable
the fear
    all-consuming
I want to know
who I am
but I am afraid to get acquainted
I am terrified to feel
and fear
I will never feel anything
again
except the fear
The trip is taking so long
twining through countless forests
of nightmares
and daytime memories
of a time
when childhood stopped
and a grownup hell began
Bumping into parts of me I never knew existed
and am reluctant to acknowledge, even now
walking
sometimes running
from
and toward
a once secure cocoon
of pain
and reluctant butterflies

           By Janice S.

♋

Beyond My Toes

Lately
Looking beyond my toes
is overwhelming
These feet want to walk backward...
escaping the fear of what's ahead
through the destructive ways of the past.
So
I spend lots of time convincing myself...
to walk ahead
and not look down
beyond my toes.

By the Motley Crew

♋

Challenging the uncertain future
By Camill

One Second

Well it's been a long time since I've
written within these pages. I guess one reason
has been fear — for I trust not — another
is that there's been lots to say, but I've
not known where to begin.
Life's been crummy as *hell* lately —
yet here I sit still struggling to survive.
Someday, maybe I'll again fulfill my dreams
of a future — but now it's one second, not
minute or day, but *second* at a time. That
seems to be all I can handle at present.

By C.L.B. and the Orchestra

♋

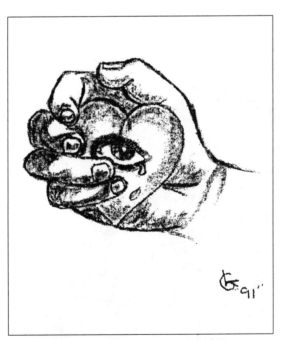

Only hope can bind the wounded heart.
By Linda G.

Somewhere, Someday, Some Dreams

Somewhere there are dreams
which will take me for a ride,
where I can drink the fresh wind
and sail freely on the breeze.
Somewhere there is a hope
that once within my reach
won't fade into futile despair,
a place to sense the softness of the rain
or be embraced by the brilliance of the sun.
Someday there will be a someone
who won't be frightened
by what they see within,
a person who can catch the moon's light
and dive beyond the dark soul's pull.
Sometime there will be a me
that can be satisfied
with the essence of who I am,
a day when there will be a peace of self
that I can truly feel and know.
But for now I'll struggle
with what I have to hold,
for that somewhere is the land of unicorns
and that someday the time of stars.

By Pseudo

♋

Scared

I don't know where I am right now
In terms of "stages of healing"
But I know I'm close and
I know this too will pass --
As you always say, Terry.
So many silent Voices have
Come forward...and I'm scared.
The suicidal thoughts and feelings
Are so strong...and I'm scared.
Will I ever get to know everyone
And everything that exists inside of me?
I don't want "integration."
Each Gift lived so that I could.
They are the reason I am sane and alive.
But I'm scared.
We've come so far
Since this Journey began...
Each rocky path seemed the worst.
But this one is by far the most hard.
I want to live!
Please hear me!
Someone inside says there are
Over 200 entities in the City in our mind.
So many now can communicate,
Cooperate, and share.
But will we ever find us all?
I'm so scared.
Somehow we've got to pull together
And heal all these painful memories..
I wish it didn't take so long.
I'm so scared.
But I have Faith, Courage and Hope.
They exist inside of me.
Even though...I'm so scared.

By D & Associates

♋

Our Walls

We were given a choice to feel pain or not to feel;
So we chose not to feel.
What we didn't know was that there was another choice,
A choice to find a real love.
So we built the walls that would protect us from pain,
but they also kept the love from passing through...
The love that is only a promised hope.
No one gave the promise I wanted.
I was afraid to hope, to want...so I didn't.
I was safe from the hurt, pain, and betrayal of trust.
Do I break down the walls or fix them?
The walls allow us to be alive
But by tearing them down we are promised a life
filled with love and peace.
Breaking down the walls would also allow the Pain in.
Is Pain the price we have to pay for Love?
Isn't pain and the promise of love the reason we chose not to feel?
I am afraid of living, not of dying; of looking back and feeling
to grieve what could and should have been,
to look ahead and hope for what is promised.
Love and Peace on Earth!
We had chosen death.
There was a sense of peace we can not explain...
And yet our walls came crashing down.
Our secrets were out. We were feeling, grieving.
We are paying the price for love.
The Pain is Deep for I is We and We are I.
I feel for all of us and all of us feel for I
It's far from done — and Peace on Earth? — It's Hell!
And yet we are *feeling* for each other and ourselves.
It's a start, we are told.
Do we dare look ahead and hope for what has been promised —
Love and Peace on Earth?!

By Mikki for the Team of Michele

♋

There Are Lines

These trees bear the ancient lines of good fortune.
The tamarack, jasper, larch and cherry
in splendid color stand 'round this field —
the heat rising up from the grass that has
held sun all day —
and now
the air is sweet with leaves at dusk.
The lines on the varied bark,
that stretches each tree up tall
and some with turns,
have formed from growth and weather.
Even storms are right in nature.

On my face
there are lines,
but not from any natural passage of weather —
no,
the lines around my eyes formed before I was old enough to speak
of what I saw, or felt, or knew.
I slipped away instead
and the lines grew deeper and deeper still.

I almost lost my eyes, mind, lungs and limb.
I died
and came back to life.

My lines are ancient like this arbor
that I lived to see,
still uncertain if I am glad.
I inhale the evening
and wish for good fortune,
or any sort of weather
that is kinder to my face.

By S.

♋

The Calling

I hear the words, like a distant screaming
wide awake — yet I must be dreaming
from rumbling growls to a high-pitch shriek
I wonder, can human voice make such speech?
I know that we're weak and our enemy's strong
So if it's saving our lives, how can it be wrong?
No longer needed — I'm given my leave
Returning to bandage — and sometimes, to grieve
for there, on the field, lie broken bodies of time
though I never knew them, I know them as mine
I'd not leave to suffer, though I'd as soon not revive
Some pieces of me, of the we that survive
                    By David T.

♋

99

Be Gentle

Be gentle with these
moments of fragile emergence
Embrace the solitude
of sadness
Trusting that the anguish
is healing
And the sorrow
will not suffocate
Be gentle with these
hours of fragile emergence
Comforting fears with
acceptance of uncertainty
Surrounded by the
solace of melody
Soothing the insanity
of doubt and denial
Be gentle with these
days of fragile emergence
Grasping for the peacefulness
so quickly disallowed
Fearfully retreating from
a gentleness not deserved.

By Cin

♋

Little One

(For Elizabeth)

Ghost of myself
Shadow of pain
Passing in stillness
Whispering

You want to scream
Your throat burns to cry out
Your eyes are the depths
Of unshed tears
Your hands are afraid to touch.

Cry, little one,
Don't be afraid.
I will stay until
The night is through.

By Megan

♋

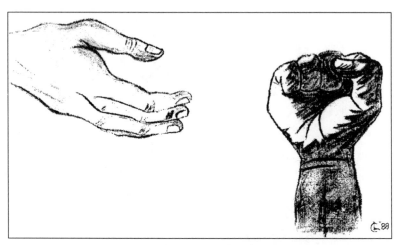

The Fist is afraid to touch.
By Linda G.

Tears

Tears are the rain of a heart that's wrapped in clouds,
Tears are the joy in a new mother's eyes;
Tears are the song of the whole world exalting,
Tears are the pride when our soul learns to fly.

Tears are the pain inside the shame that binds us,
Tears heal the hurt that makes us feel alone.
Tears speak the words our hearts can't bear to say;
Tears are a cry for help when we reap what we have sown.

Tears are the anger at a young child's dying,
Tears are a warning that someone's gone too far;
Tears are the majesty of a new dawn awakening,
Tears are the quiet in the silver evening star.

So welcome your tears, all their laughter and their sorrow,
Let your thoughts and your emotions become as one;
Remember that tears are tiny shining crystals,
And remember they make rainbows when they touch the sun.

By Steph & Cast

Tears
By ABB

Labor

The work seems so hard, and the progress feels so slow sometimes.
We wonder if we will ever feel the world. One of our many wrote this as
motivation to continue on:

Oh Father,
Why is it so hard?
The other day I picked a flower but then I had to
labor to smell it.
I saw children playing but then I had to work
to hear their joy.
I sleep but I toil to rest; it brings no relief.
I have hands to grasp, eyes to see, ears to hear.
But it is so difficult to bring it to my mind's eyes,
my body's soul.
I am not complaining, but Why?

My child, be still,
it is because you work that you have.
When you labor and join together
your hands can bring the flower's scent
to all within, your eyes can bring inside the joys of out.
Do not stop your work.
Many are still hidden in your corners,
straining to see, to hear, to feel.
If you do not work and struggle now
they will never be able to share with you
the beauties that are everywhere
and all of ours.
Rest will come
Peace is close by
But now the days must be filled
with work.

By Kathy A.

♋

103

Sheltered with His Love

It's raining outside, a slow, steady rain.
It reminds me of God's tears,
God's tears for this fallen world,
For all the pain and sadness man has caused.
But then I notice one more thing,
I'm inside and sheltered from the rain
Just as God's love shelters us
Through any kind of sadness and pain we may have.
Even though we are surrounded by this pain
God is still always there with His love.
He feels our sadness; He feels our pain;
He cries His tears along with ours.
Yet we are sheltered by His never-ending love
Always sheltered with His love.

But you may ask, "What if I'm outside,
In the rain without any shelter?
The puddles are getting deeper,
The gray sky shows no light?
Then how can you say
That I'm sheltered with His love?"
Just remember that the rain represents God's tears,
The more pain you feel, the more pain He feels.
So the puddles may be getting deeper
But that's the pain that God is in
And what better way to show His love
Than to share in our pains and fears.
So have the hope that so many have had
That one day soon all of the rain will end.
The pain and the tears will all be gone
And the shelter of God's love will shine through
Even stronger and brighter than ever before.

Even though we are surrounded by this pain
God is still always there with his love.
He feels our sadness; He feels our pain;
He cries His tears along with ours.
Yet we are sheltered by His never-ending love
Always sheltered with His love.

By Hope

Persistence

Sometimes I get so disappointed
in myself, in the events of my life
I just want to leave —
but there's too much to consider —
so I end up taking a breath and
remaining — still unsatisfied, unsettled —
yet still here.
How many long years can it be?
How many times will I have to
make the decision of my small existence?
It seems that everytime I turn around
I have to face the misplaced identities
of all my previous days —
they weigh in upon me,
a force I can't bear to keep aloft.
And so it all comes down to
my ability to uphold
the uncertainties of my past
without losing the person of now —
no easy juggling act,
as I can testify
each time I look at the damage
within myself.
But so far I've kept at it,
although I can't say how.

By Pseudo

♋

The Rock

We stand upon the granite rock
Feeling its strength beneath our feet,
Waiting impatiently for the miracle to begin.
What is this miracle we've been waiting for?

What caused us to walk that mile
So early in the morning
That now has us spellbound
Upon this granite rock?

We were driven by a force so strong
That to deny it
Would be denying all that is within us,
And all that we see and feel.

We may still be infantile with our feelings
And sense of who we are,
But we can no longer deny the essence of our beings.
We are real!

The suspense is so great
It almost overwhelms us as we stand and wait.
The rock, with its great strength
And knowledge of the past,
Not just our past, but the world's itself,
Quietly stands silent.

Suddenly, it begins its magical performance;
Which makes us feel
That we are the only ones in the audience.

The soft breeze begins to blow,
And the flowers and trees begin their soft silent dance.
They are the true dancers of the world,
And this is their chance to perform in all quietness.

The lights begin to shine.
It is the moment we've been waiting for.
The arms of the brightness reach out
To take our hands;
Soothing, safe and free.

It is non-judgmental;
Only forgiving and hopeful.
As it moves to embrace all of us,

We feel a sense of peace, hope and strength
That we seldom are able to feel.
Our body becomes enmeshed,
Never wanting for it to leave;
Wishing...hoping to be safe again.

All energy within us
Suddenly becomes at peace.
For that moment we are free.
Free of the pain of past events.
Free to be who we are
Without continual censorship of ourselves.

The light begins to hurt our eyes;
So we look away,
Only to see a shadow of one standing upon a rock.

We wonder how this can be true
When we are so many.
We wonder if it will ever be...

By The Knot, For Kim

On Mount Olympus

Though days seem dark, I dream with the gods,
Apollo, Iris and Mars...
Their laughter rings through the galaxies
And I dance among the stars.

I drink with Orion at the Milky Way,
Diana and I hunt the moon.
Orpheus shows me his palace of sleep
But Venus, the morning star, comes too soon.

Some say I live with my head in the clouds
And I march to a different drum,
But it's my dreaming song that keeps me alive,
That makes my heart-strings thrum.

In my dreams I can be whatever I want,
There's no-one to scream "It's a lie!"
I'll be serious, staid, and quiet by day,
But at night! At night, I can...fly.

By Steph and the Cast

Freedom
By Lynn W.

Integration

I am a water wheel
A hub with many spokes
Turning constantly
Spinning, without control
    Rising out of the icy water
    A spoke has barely enough time to see the sun
    Feel the warmth begin to dry its surface
    Before plunging into frothing turbulence once again
The hub does not get wet
It sits in the corner
Whipping its victims around and around
Closing its dark eyes against the dizziness
    We become mechanical
    We do our jobs without question
    We do not resent the hub
    We push away the pain of the sharp rocks
We understand our importance
Remove a spoke, and the wheels would collapse
The hub would not be able to operate the wheel
And we would all drown
    Icy water filling our lungs
    Seeping through the soft wood
    Touching our heart
    Delivering an irreversible eternal blackness
Now we live in fear
That the woodsman will come
Which spoke will he saw off first?
The pounding of his heavy boots draws near
    The stronger ones watch
    As the weaker begin to deteriorate
    Bending near breaking point in the turmoil
    The hub cannot control them
We try to cry out
But the angry people walk by and laugh
They do not understand our fear
So we spin
And spin
And wait

By Christine and Anne Marie

Who Am I?

I am four Creatures:
    Pain Creature,
    Scare Creature
    Shame Creature, and
    Little Angry Creature.

Pain Creature feels the evil and must hold still.
I must hold myself very carefully and gently,
so I don't feel disturbed and become bigger.
I freeze in space,
I freeze in time,
I freeze in process because there is no hope of pain going
away.

Pain Creature stay right there; that's right
don't breathe, don't do anything!

Scare Creature fears the evil.
I must keep moving, keep going
even when I'm tired.
My watching must never stop, the evil might be near.
My thinking must work hard to stay ahead of the evil games.
If I don't keep thinking, watching and doing, terror moves in.

Scare Creature keep running, keep looking, keep thinking,
    everywhere and anywhere.

Shame Creature hides from the world.
I hide my face, I hide my voice; no one should know about me.
I hide my body; no one should see me, or think about me.
If anyone does see, think, or know about me, he will say,
"How awful."

Hide Shame Creature; hide quickly, before it's too late!

Little Angry Creature hides from everyone and everything.
I must not be found; if I am found, I will grow so big that
nothing will be able to contain me.
I will stay hidden where nothing can upset me.
I will keep believing there is no evil, so I don't need to come out.

Keep hiding Little Angry. Keep your eyes closed
so you won't see the evil memories.

Who else am I?
I am two more Creatures:
    Brave Companion and
    Hope Companion.

Brave Companion keeps facing the evil.
I feel Pain, Scare, Shame, and Little Angry; yet I keep traveling
toward the evil of the past.
I keep opening the doors so we all can look to see who
is there, and what is there.
No matter what I see, I stay, because that is what I must
do to help Pain, Scare, Shame, and Little Angry feel better.

Keep going, Brave Companion, there are rewards ahead because
of your diligence!

Hope Companion sees the wondrous future.
I weave myself around Pain, comforting and cradling
in soft arms, telling her it won't last forever.
I am always with Scare, by her side to assure that
someday she will know that evil is gone.
I smile at Shame and say, "I can see you, and I know you.
I like you, just the way you are today, and the way
you will be in all your tomorrows."
I look Little Angry right in the eye and tell him that
I'm not afraid of him, and that some day we will
all welcome him to the meetings.

Keep the wondrous vision, Hope; we all depend on you!

Hope and Courage Companions say, *Come Pain, come Scare,*
come Shame, come Little Angry, come with us and journey into
the past. We will ask our friend, Light Companion, to go with us
and show us the way. He will help us see, feel, and remember. He
will help us find Authority and Power to conquer evil.

Power and Authority will conquer and heal.

And then my name will be:
Victory,
Peace,
Joy,
Love, and
Appreciation for my Companions.

By Beth Gassen-Parsons

Which Way Now?
By David T.

Chapter

4

Moving Closer

Maybe there's hope after all.

Normal Now

By MARY R.

When we were first diagnosed with MPD, I (Mary) was frightened of the rest of us, who had been more or less hidden inside. We were in a psychiatric hospital at the time, and while we were there I slowly got used to hearing some of the other parts come out and talk in therapy sessions. (We have a lot of co-consciousness.) Eventually I realized we'd all been working together for many years and I was "only" being asked to recognize how we've been all our lives — multiple.

Three weeks after diagnosis, we left the hospital. I was calmer and a little more able to accept some of the other parts in our system, but I also felt as if I had *Multiple Personality Disorder* in huge hot pink neon letters plastered to my forehead. I felt like a freak! I coped by thinking about *Integration* a lot. Integration might not mean I've reached the Promised Land, I told everyone, but it does mean we get to be a *Normal Person Just Like Everyone Else.*

I'd read *Diagnosis and Treatment of Multiple Personality Disorder,* by Frank W.Putnam,M.D. (with help from inside) and knew to expect three to five years from the MPD diagnosis to integration. I immediately commanded us to integrate within three years. We hoped to speed the process along by reading all the clinical literature on MPD that we could find, and unwisely bought so many books we had soon charged our credit card to its limit.

Let's see, I thought, *three years to integration...I've been diagnosed for a month...just two years, eleven months to go!* I was almost counting the seconds to *Integration.* Meanwhile, my therapist correctly insisted she had no idea how long my integration would take and *neither did I.*

Time has changed my perspective. I'm proud to say it's been thirteen months since diagnosis, which we now refer to as "our true nature being recognized." We've stayed out of the hospital and hope to never again need inpatient care for psychiatric problems.

We are much more accepting of each other now and we are beginning to work well together as a team. It's (almost) hard for me to remember how I felt when I was so frightened of learning about our system. We're just *us,* after all!

Part of accepting who we are is realizing there are many kids inside us...relatively few of us are adults. (Our biological age is 24.) Most children are 15 and younger, with *many* children seven and younger. Taking care of the kids isn't always easy, and we often mess up, but we adults try to protect the children and keep them calm and safe. We avoid triggers as much as possible (and as a satanic cult survivor, there can be *a lot* of triggers). We also do "fun kid things" like reading children's stories, playing with our Lite Brite (a children's toy), watching *Sesame Street* (especially Kermit the Frog and the Cookie Monster), blowing bubbles, playing "inside" (our head, that is), and spending time in our safe place.

Our safe place is inside an eggshell decorated on the outside with gold lines and bouquets of roses tied together with a gold ribbon. We call it "the Golden Egg." A glass oval opens when we ring a doorbell, and we walk into the egg carrying our friends, the kids' stuffed animals. Inside, the egg is beautiful. In the winter, ice and snow covers the trees and ground; cherry blossoms bloom and animals come out to play in spring; all the trees and flowers bloom in the summer, and the leaves change colors and fall to the ground in autumn. Our egg doesn't have anything to do with the real world, so we can have as many adventures as we want inside it (as long as we are safe and comfortable). Sometimes we find it hard to accept that the egg exists in our mind instead of the real world, but we usually just feel happy to have a safe place.

Another part of accepting ourselves is our rejection of the word "alter." This may sound like heresy to other MPD/DD people, but we view "alter" as an insulting word. "Alter" is short for "altered state of consciousness," and as someone said in the book *MPD From the Inside Out*, all of us are equally "real"; we are not a system with one "real" personality and other "pretend" or "less real" parts. Since we're all equally real, we feel it's unfair to designate oneself as one "normal" state of consciousness and others "altered" states of consciousness.

We also don't like to use the possessive; I don't own any other parts so I don't talk about "my" other parts or "my" multiple personalities. We prefer to say "we are many." The extensive use of the phrase "my alter(s)" in MPD/DD recovery books grates on us like the sour sound of a chord played on an out-of-tune piano. (This is a very minor complaint though — our recovery and positive attitude about ourselves would not be possible without reading other multiples' stories.) We refer to ourselves as "us" or "parts" or "the rest of us inside."

As we learned to accept ourself and all of us began to express our feelings in therapy, my/our preoccupation with integration decreased. *Why should the kids have to grow up and change if they don't want to?* we asked ourselves. *What's wrong with us the way we are?*

We realize now we're *Great* the way we are. Now we think integration isn't so important after all. We already have a lot of co-consciousness and work together as a team. Some of us are curious about how we'd turn out if we all integrated...but our system contains many parts and we try not to force some parts' ideas about integrating onto everyone. Those who want to integrate can, and the rest of us can stay just as we are, because *We're a Normal Person Now.*

♋

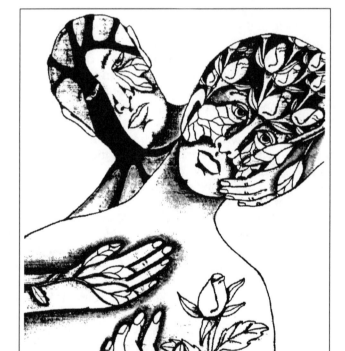

Trust
By Living Earth

Recipe for One Complete Person

1 cup shattered pieces of a personality
   1/2 a pinch of this personality
   1/2 a pinch of that personality
      3/4 of the rest of them
(Make sure to include all personalities, even if you don't like them.
Throw them in anyway.)
      Blend together on low speed
    Sprinkle with lots of feelings
   Cook however long it takes to complete therapy
      and until well done.
      (makes one serving)
   *nuts optional, but readily available
         By Julie, the Learner

Broken Child
By ABB

Nourishment

She walked to the depression in the ground
Added water, said some words
And walked away.

She returned day after day
Added water, said some words
And walked away.

Nothing happened.

She returned day after day
Added her tears, her love
And walked away.

She returned day after day
Added her tears, her love
And walked away.

Her soul grew and flourished.

By Paula Hurwitz

♋

Our Love/Hate Relationship with the Integration Process

By SUSIE & CO.

The integration process...we hate it, we love it, we don't want to deal with it, but we get excited when we make progress with it.

Integration has many meanings to us: death, pain, wholeness, confusion, isolation, productivity, non-productivity, better functioning relationships, no agreement on who to be in a friendly or sexual relationship with, happiness, sadness, celebrating life, mourning lost life/lives, hopes and dreams realized, and maybe no agreement on what hopes and dreams to work towards.

We in this body called "Susie," which is 49 years old, experienced great fear and hope at the beginning of therapy, when the stated goal of therapy was integration. There are four adults in this body who have most of the control of it, each at different times, but on and off for most of the 49 years. When one of us was in control, we were complete and independent of the others. We have different vision, physiology, sexual preferences, careers, talents, phobias, likes, dislikes, friends, social circles, etc...to name a few.

One of us is called "Susie" (birth nickname.) She may have a slight sense of more ownership of the body than the rest of us three adults, but not much. We have other adult parts (alters) but they have been in the body much less time over the years. We also have teenagers, children, two inner-self-helpers, and at least three animal alters (with very little time in the body): a horse, redtail hawk, and wolf. But we do not have a definite "host." Never have. There could be a birth personality who is dormant; we just don't know right now.

In the beginning, integration meant death to some of us. We become angry with professionals who say we are not real people or persons; we are real persons sharing one body. We've had major philosophical questions arise among ourselves Re: integration.

After several months of therapy, one of us, Liz, called our therapist and said, "How can you kill me? I've been a separate person all my life. I've just shared this body with others, but I've had a whole and healthy life all on my own. I've just borrowed this body from the others on and off through the 49 years." So, even thinking about integration as it was thought of one to three years ago brought extreme fear to us and mostly not the hope it was meant to instill.

In the beginning, Susie was feeling as if she was probably the host, so integration gave her some hope. This soon turned to fear when she realized how different the rest of us were from her, how much influence we had, and how we all gained easy and complete control of the body.

Soon, three of the four main parts, Susie, Lexi, and Liz, were in extreme fear of integration. The fourth part, CiCi, was in denial of the others' existence at this time; working towards the goal of integration was not even an issue for her. She denied the others and the existence of MPD. When she happened to hear one of our voices, which was not often, she feared it meant she was insane and she was making our voices up.

When our therapist would try to point out the obvious indicators of our presence, such as lost time, ending up some place she didn't remember going to, wearing clothes she never put on or bought, etc., she would just panic and feel crazier, because she thought she should be able to remember those things.

We all had to do hard work at just integrating CiCi into our system. It has not been easy for us or our therapist, Dr. B. After 1-1/2 years of work, she was in denial about 20% of the time, and in pain, fear and feeling suicidal all the time. We didn't want her in our system because she was filled with toxic shame and self-hate, and was suicidal. We are very grateful for the patience and loving care of our beloved Dr. B., who gave us hope and safety through this process. Now, we have better communication between us and CiCi, both ways. She also journals sometimes, and participates in therapy.

Our process towards integration has meant that some of our adult parts who have not had a lot of time in the body over the 49 years, have somewhat, if not completely, fused with the four main adult parts. CiCi has taken the role of an adult since our body was in its teens, so we refer to her as an adult — but she is closer to age twelve or thirteen.

Part of our process of integration has meant hard and constant work towards greater communication, cooperation, consideration and compassion, of and with one another. We call this *The Four C's*. It has meant a lot of journaling, quiet time, sharing of the body, etc., and something as simple (and difficult) as wearing each others' clothes, being polite to each others' friends, accepting each others' reality, having respect for one another, acknowledging each other privately and publicly (when safe.) We also work on having more control over switching and hopefully not being totally at the mercy of environmental factors/triggers.

At this time, integration meant simply integration into the system of all parts who make up the whole of those who inhabit the body called "Susie."

Gradually, the adults started to have a different sense of what final integration would mean to us. We are now working towards what we call *Natural Integration*. Our process consists of sharing memories, experiences, obtaining as close to 100% co-consciousness and co-presence as possible. We trust that our mind, heart and body will be the best guide during the process, and when enough of our goal has been met for us to start functioning as "normal" as possible, have productive and happy lives, we will consider the majority of our integration work done. We will intuitively know when the time comes.

Our therapist, Dr. B., and God, have been our main guides on this healing journey. We view this as a process that will continue to one degree or another as long as we live.

We have very strong feelings against "forced integration" and/or "hypnotized integration." We believe that forcing a process to move along faster than the mind/body is ready to deal with it, is the main cause of integration "failures."

Also, we take issue with therapists who rush to integrate parts (alters) who are highly suicidal, chemically dependent, etc., with a host who is not strong enough at the time to handle the constant influence of these parts. In this case, the host can become extremely suicidal or chemically dependent herself or himself. We've heard of therapists who push for this because they think it will considerably dilute the strength of the acting-out parts, thus making it easier to control acting out. We have found it makes more sense to work with these parts separately in therapy, and have the stronger parts support and nurture them as much as possible. For us, it has been easier to contain our suicidal part when she is integrated into our system, but not fused with one of us. We've seen fellow M.P.'s lives become totally unmanageable when a therapist has felt that fusing a suicidal part to the host would diminish or end acting-out, when in reality the problem is exacerbated. The host is even more overwhelmed and in a sense, two parts end up acting-out.

We are experiencing sadness and concern that after 49 years of great separateness, it appears as though we will probably never be one whole person or "sole proprietorship." But we will be grateful for the opportunity to become a high functioning "limited partnership," rather than the unwieldy "conglomerate" we have been!

We also accept that we will never be 100% healed, because healing means working on spiritual and psychological healing. For us this is a lifelong process, and in some ways a linear time frame is not even involved.

Last but not least, part of mending ourselves means doing our part to mend the earth, help fellow M.P.'s mend, and to pray daily for the healers who help to mend M.P.'s . Integration is not just an "inside job." Our integration must include integration with humanity, the earth, and the universe.

Our room at home.
Drawn with help from our
external friend K.

Come Into My Arms

Come into my arms
precious child
Reach with trembling weariness
for a place where there is
breath without fear
Where loneliness is but
a memory
Where the violation and suffocation
of an embrace
Becomes a gentle touch of
comfort and presence
Come into my arms
precious child
Reach with trembling weariness
for a time when the eternity
of abandonment is only a
moment of solitude
When the terror of shadows
and darkness fades forever
into the sunrise
When your existence is no longer
a punishment
But is celebrated, treasured,
and cherished.
Come into my arms
precious child.

By Cin

♋

The Ring

By SONYA ROGERS

I was diagnosed about two years ago and I've noticed a pattern that has developed. It seems that I have this group of alters called The Ring and, one by one, each comes out with a little more anger and memories than the one before. The first one, Danielle, was somewhat bitter, and a good dancer. After she did some hard work and learned some healthy socialization skills, she "laid down" with me.

Then Two came. Actually, we became consciously aware of her, but didn't "witness" her until Danielle was beginning to settle down. After Danielle "merged," Two really appeared on the scene. Now Two was like Danielle when it came to the initial resistance, but there were some differences. She didn't have Danielle's Southern speech and Two was twice as "pissed off." Two had very good organizational skills because her job was to make sure the system stayed in line and no one (outside) would get close enough to hurt anyone.

Then after much hard work, the system said that they can hardly tell the difference between me and her. I don't know if we've integrated, but she's not as angry, somewhat likes to socialize, and we don't go by separate names.

And *now* there's another one on the scene. She says her name is Nobody. This has only happened within the last two or three weeks, so it's still new to us. She says that she was part of The Ring, and she was "forced" out like Danielle and Two. She says that The Ring would band together and decide who would "surface" almost like a group of kids getting together and pushing someone out of the group to do a task that really no one wanted to do, and then they all sit and watch to see what happens.

I'm not aware of how this process takes place because I wasn't a part of The Ring. All I have is what Two and Nobody say. Nobody is full of pure rage. She has called our therapist horrible names and has caused minimal damage to her things and us. She does threaten to do worse, but nothing's happened yet. Nobody sits in a very sexual position, but I think it's more of a statement of the abuse than a request or command. She has challenged our therapist. She says she will do her best to force our therapist to "fire" us and prove the abusers right. (The old tapes about "You're disgusting. No one will ever like you.") Our therapist has accepted her challenge and says she will prove the abusers wrong.

I have a lot of fear around wondering what Nobody is going to do. She has so much rage. Our therapist has proven to us that she can control Nobody and The Ring by holding the kids before Nobody comes out. She has this way of holding our arms in a nonthreatening way and when Nobody or The Ring surfaces and fights to run or do damage, our therapist keeps a firm grip and prevents them from running out. This helps us to feel safer, and to be honest, I think Nobody and The Ring feel safer from themselves even though they struggle very hard to get away. (Of course, they would never admit this.)

It seems that this Ring was created long ago to preserve my anger. Even though I'm appalled at their behavior and the awful pictures they give us of what they will do to this body, I am grateful for their courage and responsibilities in my life. My therapist keeps reassuring me that I'm not "certifiably committable," and these things will be worked out. She has a very strong belief in her God, and I'm glad because usually I borrow some of her strength when mine takes a little vacation.

♋

Adulthood Integrated

Survived the unsurvivable.
Lived a divided life.
Trying to believe the unbelievable.
Accept a divided self.

Gather the fragments of memory.
Look at them in the light.
Take in.
Let go.
Move on.

By The Company

The Guardian, by Jesse
For Steph & the Cast

Not Alone

I walked alone
confused and weary
A voice spoke
It scared me
She said *Don't worry*
I have come to help
We often talked
No names involved
All I knew was
I wasn't alone anymore
After time others came
We were confused
The world around us
Was very different
Than the world in us.
We kept speaking inside
Our comfort found there
We were not crazy
Just different than others
The fear stayed as though
We knew a secret kept
Must keep you safe
Then more and more came
We knew we must band together
To face the strange world
We must help each other to stay safe.
Now we are a community inside.
Safe in each other's arms.

By Stacy Joy

♋

In A Room

In a room that felt unfamiliar
Our eyes met
Then for some reason the room didn't feel
so unfamiliar any more.
We did not talk,
But through our eyes we knew
that we were friends.
With our eyes we communicated,
With our smile we assured
that there was safety in this friendship.
The weeks went by,
and the unfamiliar room was not
unfamiliar anymore
Our eyes were not unfamiliar anymore,
For they spoke a silent language,
that only you and I understood.
Soon the friendship grew stronger
and only the hidden secrets
we were too afraid to share.
But now my friend,
we are free to share these hidden secrets.
Our friendship has grown,
Our trust has grown.
My dear friend, I love you.

By Yvonne and Friends

♋

Justification

Your existence no longer
has to be justified, nor do
those feelings you hold
inside, either to yourself
or to others. Just your
striving to live, the focus
being your true inner-self,
is justification
...without explanation.

By Debbie 32

♋

Cooperation
By Mary S.

The Fragile Haven

By RAE

Within the glass exterior of her body there dwelled a haven of Ones.

Ones that pushed to the very north and south and east and west of their confines. Throughout the very breadth of the glass body they existed.

Beings within arms' reach of one another, but never touching; within speaking distance but never breaking the silence.

The body was cracking. The glass had splintered in places and many feared for their lives, but still they did not reach out.

At times, for brief moments, it was thought that the sound of children's voices could be heard. But everyone knew that was ridiculous, because all the Ones were forbidden to speak. Yet, the very hint of those sounds seemed to keep the glass body from shattering further.

The moistness of tears and cries kept the body nourished, and the knowledge of the world seen through their visible panes served to keep the Ones from breaking up in despair, and death coming upon the girl of glass.

Everyday Ones after Ones came to the heart of the splintered body. Each holding its own shard, they tried to fit it into its place of origin, hoping to breathe life into their rapidly deteriorating enclosure.

Now as always, the quiet sound of the child voice could be felt throughout and within. And it kept the Ones hopeful and following. The sound was growing in strength and its mournful, wistful song was weaving its way throughout the north and the south and the east and the west of the city of Ones.

They began to reach out to try to touch the sound and take it within. In their attempts they laid hands upon hands, they pressed ears to lips and began to speak and share as one.

As hand began to touch hand and lips pressed to ears a strong blue light began to infuse throughout the fragile haven of Ones.

And they were warmed by it, and nurtured and strengthened.

The incessant need to find a place for their glass shard within the heart seemed to lessen, and it in turn began to draw each One to it freely.

The heart grew strong and fulfilled by the many's glass pieces and its beats became rhythmic in sound and echoed within and without the strengthening being.

Its life force enveloped everyone, from the smallest of the small to the biggest of the big; to the hostile, to the mournful, to all the Ones. And they felt as a family. Their breaths in unison, the body strengthened.

Blue light came to fuse the cracks, but one crack was left. A reminder for the Ones to see what had been and remember. And with the remembering came a knowledge and love within and throughout for each and the other.

They loved, and the girl of glass was then loved and whole. She was able to stand and walk and play and be. And the Ones were happy and peacefilled.

The Ones were amazed, that through their unity and sharing this girl of glass could do all this and more, and no one or anything could come and shatter the glass haven that was theirs, ever again.

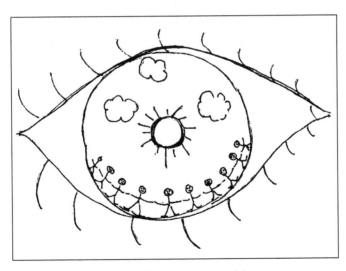

Looking at my world.
By Heather

The Seething

Something inside will not
    remain mine.
A voice demanding an audience.
I am only the instrument
    available to recite the
    jailed message.
Releasing these muffled thoughts
Through words alive bubbling
    in the cauldron.
Vibrations of restlessness...

By DST

Howling out the pain.
By Daile

Lena

Don't say her name.
It will contaminate, pollute
untie the knots of sense and logic.
She isn't one of us, no connection.
Lock her up — take her away.
We can't stand to see
her emerald eyes, dangerous eyes
full of riotous longings
defined in 3-D
and carnival-colored prisms
to draw us in, betray our guilt.

Shameless libertine
smelling of summer musk
and daisies chained in ebony hair
she is our leper
our shy and bold Adonis rose
red-striped with menarche stains
and woman-pains.
She can't be us — she can't be me.

What devil's advocate is this
who sets her free
proclaims her real, brave enough
to learn new rules for growing up
like verse becoming poetry.

She can't be me — and yet
the mirror blurs, spinning bits of light
and mystery. I can't escape.
Pubescent still, she claims my soul
and I am Lena, after all.

By Janice B.

♋

Welcome

Welcome back all of you
to my awake consciousness

My life without knowing each of you
was one shadowed by loneliness

The journey to find all of you
has sometimes been one of unpleasantness

The memories of some of you
were consumed with anger and painfulness

While others of you
bring total happiness

As I accept and welcome each of you
I rejoice in the freedom of growing wholeness

By Melody Sue McCurry

Self

The relation of self is gone
Leaving in its quake a feeling of loss.
Sure, there are many roles to be played
But who is the true self?
The teacher — so self-assured
Or a poet with words flowing freely
Then there's the artist — creative to a 'T'
And what of the mommy — the one who loves?
Yes! all are parts of me.
Yet! question is: Who am I inside?
You know, down where the feelings are
The inner self that's longing for a life of its own.
Am I the child so insecure that needs mothering
Or the adult — standing tall — walking beside you?
Not in front nor behind — being led along
But rather beside as an equal — not leaning.
Yet! self is gone — I know not who I am
Or what role I play anymore.
Securities are shifting — needs changing
Where does that leave me — within?
Help me find a self inside
But this time a self I can be proud of.
Don't let me drown in the quake of loss
Guide me — don't lead me down the path,
One full of newness of self
Walk beside me as an equal
Not leading me like a child.

By C.L.B. and the Orchestra

♋

Integration, Getting Ready

By SALLY/SHIRLEY

From Shirley's Journal
3/16/93

Today I realized I believe in the reality of being a multiple personality. I was driving my husband home from his doctor's appointment in the next community, and I was telling him what it is like for me, being multiple.

It was easier for me to tell him after I had told a friend what it is like. This friend is from my support group. Telling other people helps me believe this strange situation myself.

An example of what being multiple is like for me, was when I said hello to my counselor in the hall after my support group meeting. He recognized one of my alters by her facial expressions and the way she moved. I was not even aware that she was out. I am not aware of the changes when they occur.

I guess I am what is called co-conscious, because I observe the alternate when we are in my counselor's office, and now I realize that each alternate personality is a part of me, but I am unable to *be* that part. For instance, one of my personalities, I think, would do all right just on her own. Sometimes I wish I could be that person all the time.

But in considering the rest, some just don't have completeness. I need them and they need me, and the others. We need to support each other, like a support group, only more so.

At my counselor's suggestion, my alternate personalities and I do a mental exercise where we all stand in a circle and give each other support, arm in arm. Also, I have been telling them I want them with me all the time. When I speak to any one of them now, they seem to be right here with me. But we are still separate. We are working toward unity.

We like the word *unity* better than *integration*. Unity may be the same as integration, but words are different for a reason. *Joining* is another word not so fearsome. And *unifying* is different, less drastic than integration. I feel all my personalities are essential. I don't want to lose any of them, especially the children.

If there is some way to integrate while keeping all the children as a whole, we would like that. Being whole is what we want — whole and united.

We would like to hear what other multiples want and how they feel about integration.

℥

Personality Party
By Stacy Joy

Treasure Hunt

My hand in a child's
I face the unwanted truth
my truth
healing truth
reclaiming truth
the core of me shattered
scattering pieces
through time
abandoned
by necessity
finally
it is time
to bring them all home
to find my bones

Lost here
lost there
slowly found
placed into the whole
the pattern of self emerges
bound by web lacing
of pure nerve
and determination
to survive.

My bones
hidden for safe keeping.
Treasures claimed
to be exclaimed over
grieved over
integrated
into the existing framework
that is self.
Howling
singing
sobbing
the bones flesh out
woman emerges
and the laughter begins
by trusting the child.

By Daile

Magic Wand

By NANCY L.

One day I found this magic wand in a toy store, and the children bought it for our therapist (sometimes they like to play with a toy or hold a teddy bear in sessions). All the inner children like to tip the wand, and watch the colored rocks tumble and fall in the water. My therapist said it was a good symbol for me/us.

The rocks are like my "people" inside — separate, yet together, forming a whole and complete wand. And I am like the water holding all the pieces together. He told me to think of myself as the water — clean, clear, bright, white, and good (not dirty and bad anymore). Now I think of MPD as a creative and "magical" way to survive.

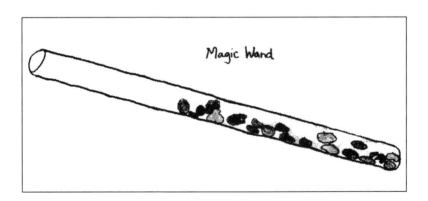

Magic Wand

Reasons to Survive

We do this for ourselves — for the child that we used to be. The child who could run and yell and laugh and cry in spite of the pain that she was hiding.

We do this in order that we may become a whole — not scattered into many parts.

We do this because we know that we are no longer alone.

We do this because God has given us the courage to face what we have become and to be more than we hoped to be.

We do this to help others plant the seed that is within them and to watch that seed take hold and sprout.

We do this for the children who are being hurt as we were hurt. They must know that there is hope for them. That hope comes through our own recovery.

We do this for the love of ourselves that has been lost.

We do this for those who continue to listen to us. They took our hand without hesitation when we reached out for help. They deserve to know that we will do our best to become healthy.

We do this for our daughter.

We do this for you. We love all of your faults and struggles and pain and anger and sadness and joy and beauty. You are the force that helps us continue.

By Janet

♋

The Difference in Me

By ELEXIS for AD/ISO

The first difference, as you can obviously see, is that sometimes I get to call myself *me* instead of *us*.

It's been almost one year since I started to see a therapist on a regular basis. (I say *see* because on many days, that's all I'm able to do. Sometimes, I just can't talk, and sometimes I find it a little hard to listen.)

Even so, over the past year, I have indeed noticed differences in me:

My ultra-painful headaches have diminished into "normal" headaches. They aren't as often, and aren't as long.

My memory has improved. On bad weeks, I have special ways to make sure that I remember. I am not missing important things as much as I used to.

I'm not nearly as afraid of people and things, like I was last year. Mostly, I am beginning to feel more comfortable with myself, and feeling more confident about this and people and things in my life.

This year I'm *seeing* more. I am not *missing* as much in life as I used to. My children aren't saying, "Don't you remember?" as much.

My life and house are more organized, as is my formerly-confused mind.

I've developed a "stick to it" attitude, not dropping everything in the middle. Finally I've begun to finish some things I've started. It takes time, but at least the attitude is better. I think that's because I remember what I've started, so I remember to finish it.

Lately, even though I'm not perfect, I feel good about myself. Before going to therapy there were many times that I've actually hated myself. Now, I tolerate the me that I am uncomfortable with, and focus on ways to change the parts that I don't like.

For more than seven or eight years, I've known that there was something wrong with me. I didn't know what it was, I just know that it was scary. I was too afraid to get what people call *professional help*. So for that many years, I've tried to talk myself into going for help. I was afraid that if I told anyone else (besides my best friend) what I felt like, that they would put me in an institution. Then one day, "Ad" tried to cut my arm with a razor. Then I knew that I couldn't wait any longer.

I'm glad that I didn't wait any longer. I might not have been here.

Much of my *difference* has to do with the help I get from my best friend, who I have known for a million years. And the rest of the difference comes from two other directions:

1. Having God back in my life (things seem to really mess up when I forget about God), and

2. Having the right therapist — the right one for me.

Even though I was very scared and very skeptical at the beginning, I knew that I was in the right place after the first couple of weeks. There were weeks when I wondered why I was going there, but I kept going back. I knew that it was helping. Even when my weeks were ultra-bad, and ultra-uncomfortable, I knew that little by little, I was seeing an improvement. That was enough for me, to keep me going back.

As "Ad" would say, it was "more good than bad."

Now, I know that it wasn't bad at all; I was just frightened.

In the past, I've never been allowed to be *me*. That is why I split into so many different pieces. Splitting thousands of times, thousands of ways, to please hundreds of people and many abusers, caused me to believe that I could never just be *me*. Now I've learned that I can be *me*, and that is just the person who I need to be!

No, I am not completely 100-percent together yet, but I am on my way. I know what it feels like to be close to 100-percent together, and that too isn't as scary as I thought it would be.

Thanks, "lo," for letting me be *me*.

In a while, I'll have a different name, my own real name. But for now, I'll just say — see you later.

♋

Rhyme for Mending

Journeys toward endless horizons,
Willows that weep as they may,
Bridges that cross to Tomorrow,
Lilies to show us the way.

Streams that gurgle before us,
Ponds that dream thru the rain,
Tears encased in a waterfall,
Caverns that shelter the pain.

Sun that sets like an ending,
Dawn that begins each new day,
Smiles embraced by a rainbow,
Laughter that beams like a ray.

Love that seems never-ending,
Hearts that here always stay,
Time that carries us onward,
Forever's a place, so they say.

By NRK

♋

Metaphysical Alter
By Dale

Where I've Been,
Where I'm Going

By SANDRA J. HOCKING

As I reflect on the past four years, from the time of my first flashback to the present, I am able to see the strides I have made in my healing.

In the beginning I was in so much pain. I look over my journals and see doubt, terror and denial joined together in a frenzied dance. The sickening roller-coaster of "yes, it happened; no, it didn't" is a common thread that rides the pages, written by many hands.

Belief that "it" happened came hard for me. Denial was a constant companion, whispering refusals in my ear.

I was often frustrated with the slowness of therapy and with the clinical detachment of my therapist. My inner children needed to be held and nurtured, which he, on principle, refused to do.

I wanted more than "sit-and-talk" therapy. I wanted to *feel* what had happened to me, not just *know* it through an alter's memory. It wasn't the same. The abuse never really became mine, but to this day remains theirs. Theirs.

Groups helped, going to workshops and conferences helped. Friends helped. Therapy helped too. But mostly, it was just me, putting one foot in front of the other.

Riding the roller-coaster, I learned that the abuse that belonged to my alters, belonged to me too. Even if I couldn't feel it, it was mine. It happened. It happened to me.

When I first began to make contact with the others who live inside me, I was terrified. Sybil, Eve, crazy, crazy, crazy. But of course, it wasn't insane at all. Choosing multiplicity was rational, sane and necessary.

The others kept me alive, kept me sane, kept me functional.

I began to know them, listen to them, trust them. And as I learned to trust these other parts of myself, I discovered I could trust myself, too.

I began to stay "present" during stressful situations. I learned to say "No," and "Let me think about it," before committing myself to outside tasks. Time loss became less and less frequent; the Voices grew quieter.

Somewhere along the line, I got tired. I got frustrated and I got bored. I was sick of seeing abuse everywhere I looked, tired of focusing on incest and its survivors, and bone-weary of my own memories.

It happened. And it happened to me. So, let's get on with it. I got tired of wallowing in the muck, and handhold by toehold, pulled myself out.

Along the way, I've written. I wrote stories and articles, poems and fears and dreams. I wrote conversations and letters and even a book. I cannot imagine healing without being able to write. Words are the one thing I could hold on to, the one thing that kept me grounded. Words kept me sane.

So, am I healed now? Am I all better? Has the Great Cosmic God of Recovery kissed my wounds and made them all better?

No.

Am I better than I was?

Yes.

I still have plenty to do. My alters, though quiet now, are still with me, and that's fine with me. I feel no need to integrate, knowing they are joined with me now, but can separate out to help me if they need to.

It's a long road that has no turning, so the saying goes. My foot is still on the path. But now I know there are shady, peaceful resting places along the way.

♋

A Vision for You

By CLAUDIA KURIC

Imagine this:

A baby girl is born. Her talents, love and passion for life are already within her, like a seed waiting to grow into a flower. As she looks around the world she's been born into, she discovers with horror that she's been placed in a war zone. Her strongest asset is her will to live. Even though she is just a baby she develops her will into a power which she uses to survive.

And she does survive. She spends her childhood doing that which will keep her alive. She lives so long in the war that she forgets she is in a war; it feels like this is what life is and will always be.

Finally, she grows older and escapes the war. She learns to cope in the outside world, but always through the eyes of a shell-shocked survivor, haunted by the ghastly terrors she lived through. Still the flower waits.

Slowly, the woman-child begins to feel her wounds and realizes something is terribly wrong. She sees that a lot of children are born into peace and allowed, even encouraged, to grow. She realizes she is still feeling the shell-shock from the war.

Thus, she begins the journey to find herself. It is a very long trip, almost unbearable at times. Along the way there are glimmers of hope, people who love her — people who actually want to support the talents and passion within her, people who want nothing in return.

After a long time the journey does get easier. And she sees that the reward for the journey is herself—all of her parts coming together in a beautiful rebirth of the person she was born to be, intended to be, had she been born into peace and love. She chooses the talents she wants to grow and becomes herself. Finally, one day, she is outside under the warm sun, the wind blowing through her hair, standing on a rock, and she announces to the clear sky, "Yes, this is me. I was born to be who I am now. I am alive, I am free, and the journey has been worth it."

This is the vision I give to you, the vision that can come true.

Co-creation,
Cooperation
By Living Earth

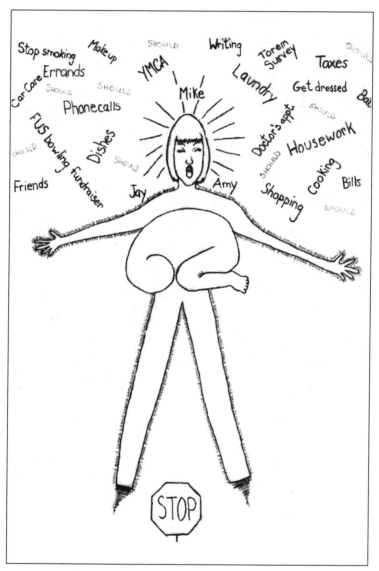

More shoulds than I can handle.
By Mary

Chapter

5

Stories of Integration

On the brink of recovery

Saying Goodbye

Goodbye
to all of you
who peopled my body
and took over my pain

When I was hurt
you stepped in
laid your life down for me

You shed my tears
bled from my body
You even loved for me

Thank all of you
for the hard and the good times
We're integrating now

I'll uniquely be
you and you'll be more me
United we stand
over child abuse.

By Beth Moore

♋

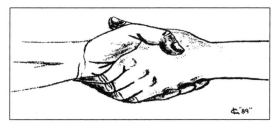

Clasping
By Linda G.

Mending Myself

By SUSAN et al

It has been almost four years since I was diagnosed with MPD and I have slowly come to realize that these have been the most extraordinary years of my life. I fought this diagnosis *hard*. I think my therapist spent the first year just trying to convince me he was right. So many things that I had decided would never have answers... "Who bought that dress? It isn't my style!" "Why can't I go down in the cellar and do the laundry without feeling two steps from hysterical?" "Why do people say sometimes when they telephone me I speak to them in a child's voice?" "And why oh why do I keep losing time?" I once woke up in bed with a man I didn't know, but boy did he seem to know me! Losing time...what a strange term. Does that mean I'll find it one day? "Yes," my doctor replies. "In a manner of speaking... integration will give you all the lost time back." I'm still not sure whether this is just his wishful thinking or a genuine possibility.

The day the psychiatrist told me I was a multiple I ripped at my arms with my fingernails to get the "others" out. I felt as though there were alien beings living inside and off me and I wanted them *out*. Slowly, painstakingly, the doctor coaxed the many, many, *many* child alters out. Perhaps that is why I remain so high functioning. There were very few adult alters to interfere or plot against one another, but boy when they did! Sometimes I think the doctor got lost in his affection for the little ones, like daughters he knew he'd never have. We were people pleasers, born psychics, and would switch to give him whatever alter he would be most comfortable with at a session.

We began to age. Little ones moved from childhood to adolescence inside a forty-year-old body. We took our first shower, all of us, together, with the bathroom door soundly locked and my husband standing just outside. Most of us had previously considered ourselves too dirty to deserve cleanliness. After all, hadn't Momma said we were bad and dirty?

We had our first night's sleep...all of us. Having slept for almost forty years with at least one alter wakefully on guard, we had never truly understood the meaning of a good night's sleep until that moment.

We adults made love to our husband of twenty-one years. Some of us were virgins, some prostitutes, all of us learned what making love meant that night. It had not been what Momma said it was.

We changed jobs, got overwhelmed, got the hang of things, made mistakes, ran for cover, got coaxed back out and started over again, just like "single people." Our little ones learned how to play, saw Bambi for the first time and decorated a Christmas tree. Money stopped flowing through our hands like water, checks stopped bouncing, bill collectors stopped calling. We stopped being afraid of the telephone.

We had setbacks. Momma died without apologizing. Her death denied us the eventual confrontation we had planned. Our relatives demanded we stay away from the funeral for having told those terrible lies about such a good woman. We went back on medication, we tripled our weekly therapy visits. We fought with the doctors, our husband, our children, our dogs, our cats. We were almost fired. We went to church. We learned to talk to God. We talked, screamed, yelled, cried. Our Reverend and our therapist held a ceremony of absolution for us, cleansing away with holy water whatever sins we believed we'd committed. We began to think we might be worth loving.

The Big Secret was told. The world didn't end, although it almost did for awhile. The doctor cried with us but still loved us. Everyone let him hug us...a major step, we hugged back. The job improved. We got a raise. Many alters voluntarily merged with their more dominant "partner." They had been waiting for years just to tell their particular secret and once told were satisfied. We have recorded each of their names and memories so that whoever is left at the end of this process will remember we were once all here. We are close to the end of the road now. Still many abreactions to engage in, still many children left to merge. Trying to be careful of those unexpected psychological potholes, still occasionally thinking of cutting to release the pain, still occasionally thinking of suicide to end this hard work. The occasions grow...more occasional.

To those at the beginning of this long and winding road we say, "It's worth it," but the truth is you're going to feel like hell for quite awhile. You will have to truly face the darkness you've been running from if you ever want to find the light. It will not be easy. If you cannot forge a true alliance with your therapist *find another one!* You will not get well without making an alliance with someone, trusting someone for the first time. Co-consciousness will mean "really" experiencing the summer heat, "really" experiencing the flu, "really" experiencing sadness. There was something truly wonderful about having an alter who was responsible for handling our colds. She's gone now and we have all learned how to sneeze without blowing our nose off. Accidentally cutting your finger will no longer mean losing four days, but you're going to "feel" that cut. Given the other possibilities, I guess we'd rather feel the sting of the cut.

You will doubt yourself, again and again and again. Prepare your therapist for reassuring you hundreds and hundreds of times. Do not apologize for needing that reassurance. You're just making up for lost time, lost years that should have been filled with the natural reassurance an adult offers a child. You deserve to be reassured and hugged and loved and comforted. You even deserve occasional bouts of serious self-pity but don't let it go on too long. It's exhausting.

Dissociation probably came naturally to you; it was easy. Reassociating will be much harder. Hang on, hang on. Others have walked the same road and lived to talk about it. Though four years ago I never thought I'd live to write these words, for all the pain, the tears, the lost friends who couldn't handle it, the mistakes, the horror, the shame, the abreactions, the undesirable alters, for all this and more...it was worth it just to be able to open my eyes each morning and not dread the start of another day. Despite how it all began, despite how horrible it was, I can now honestly say...life is good.

♋

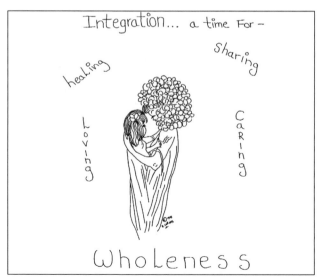

By Abigail Collins

When I felt very much trapped inside my body, wishing I could just find the zipper and get the hell out, an art therapist suggested I do some work around this image. What resulted feels more like a metaphor for the process of recovering from multiplicity — including the fear of looking inside, grieving over the loss of separate personalities as they are integrated, and the emerging of the core personality which now embodies everyone. I think where I am in my process is depicted in picture #2, becoming aware that there are inner guys, trying to establish communication and cooperation so that we can work together.

By KRK

Thanks to Everyone

By LAURA

Shoot. I don't know who to address this letter to. Addressing it to "the kids" just doesn't feel right. Yes, you may have been children, and yes I may have grouped you as "the kids" to protect myself, but you each had your own individual contributions which were of great consequence. So, Mandy, Andy, Billie, Beth, Betsy, Frankie, Alexandria, Elizabeth, and Nicky, this letter is for you. I won't forget you. Thank you for doing what was necessary to protect me and keep me safe.

I don't want you to feel that I don't appreciate your own individual contributions, which was what Frankie felt when I started counting down how many more kids I had left to integrate yesterday. I grouped you together as "the kids" because it was easier for me to see you as a group, instead of individuals. I'm sorry if this hurt you. I was overwhelmed by the number of parts that I had to integrate. Unfortunately, I didn't take the time to see how this affected you. I was only aware of things when they affected me. When I integrated Alexandria, I discovered that my shortsightedness helped me to survive. But I'm still sorry that I hurt you. I want you all to know that I know each one of you had your own contributions, and that I needed each one of you to survive. Thank you for being there for me. You were always there when I needed you, no matter what I needed.

Even in this letter, I'm grouping you all together. So before I continue, I want to take the time to thank each of you individually for what you did:

Mandy: Thank you for storing my childhood hopes and dreams.When we integrated, I received knowledge and feelings from my early childhood. You helped me manage all that was happening to me, so that I didn't become overwhelmed. I couldn't have kept growing without separating from my hopes and dreams. Thank you for staying a child, so that I could become an adult.

Andy: You were the best big brother a girl could ask for. You were always trying to figure out what I could do differently so that I could minimize the abuse. Thank you for watching out for me.

Billie: You maintained my inquisitive nature. Curiosity was not a safe attribute to have. It caused me to get into more trouble than necessary. Thank you for carrying my inquisitiveness, so it wouldn't be lost.

Beth: You carried my need to be held and comforted. Early on, I learned that the only way anyone would hold me was in a sexual way, so my need to be held and comforted had to be safely tucked away. Thank you for taking this need, so I could do what I had to do to survive.

Betsy: You carried the acknowledgment that sometimes I felt weak. Whatever I faced, no matter what I felt, I couldn't let anyone know. I had to be strong. Staying in bed all day just was not an option. Thank you for staying in bed, so that I could get out.

Frankie: You carried my opinions. Having an opinion was not safe. In order to survive, I had to become almost pliant. Whatever they wanted, I had to let happen. Having opinions threatened my survival, because it was too easy to say "fuck you," which was not exactly the best thing to say. Thank you for protecting me from myself.

Alexandria: Knowing and feeling things that didn't directly affect me was dangerous. As a child, I learned that if one paid attention, there was a distinct pattern and order. Determining that order was necessary for my survival, but I had to learn that no matter how hard I tried I could only take care of myself. Thank you for helping me pay attention to what affected me. I wouldn't have survived, if I tried to ensure that everyone else did.

Elizabeth: At first my parents' behavior towards me seemed normal to me. I didn't know any other way. Once I started seeing how other parents interacted with their kids, I became confused, distrustful, and ashamed of how my parents treated me. Since I depended on my parents for survival, this caused problems. Thank you for taking my confusion away, so that I could accept their behavior as normal.

Nicky: Regardless, if their behavior was normal or not, it pissed me off. They hurt me and in general treated me badly. Thank you for isolating me from my anger. I got into enough trouble without the added tensions that my anger would have brought.

One of the things that makes me ashamed is that since I grouped you together as "the kids," I made light of your contributions. I mean — you were children. What could you really have done? I know now that the answer is *A lot.* I can't believe that I treated you so badly, and that you let me. I guess it shouldn't be that much of a surprise that you didn't say a word. You were there to protect me, and until I was ready to acknowledge your roles you did what you had to do. I am sorry that my short-sightedness discounted you. Thank you for not losing sight of the fact that you loved me. It would have been so easy for you to say *"Fine. You deal with it."* Thank you for letting me be where I needed to be.

You all did so much. You were so strong, and I'm the one who is left. Oh, I realize that everyone is a part of me now and we are together, but the injustice saddens me. Each and every one of you deserved to truly have your own life. Instead, you chose to integrate with me because as when you were created, you knew that I needed you. Even when I was scared and tried to prevent the integrations, you all knew that I needed you to go on to the next step and did everything in your power to make the integrations feel safe to me. I'm honored by your love. Thank you.

I know that as times changed, so did your roles. When the body was a child, you stayed inside the system and hardly ever came out. But when things started getting to be too much for me in present-day life, you started coming out to relieve some of the pressure. I enjoyed having you out. It was nice to watch you having fun instead of always being weighed down in all the pain and what needed to be done. It gave me hope for the future. Thank you for showing me that life could still be fun.

I will miss you, but I'm also looking forward to what we will do together. We were a great team when we were separate. I think that we will be unbeatable now that we are together again. I look forward to discovering things that I enjoy.

I love you and thanks again,
Laura

♋

ALTERations

Does life end, I postulate
When all of us must integrate?
That's a question I dare not ask
Until I understand the task.

Will I be first or maybe last?
When will you take away my past?
Will I grow up before I go,
Or is that something you don't know?

Will I never think again,
All my writing at an end?
Will Paula be the only one
To see the stars and feel the sun?

I do not want to go away;
This is my life and here I'll stay.
I do not want to be her part.
I have a soul; I have a heart.

Take the others, all so bland,
I'd miss them less than grains of sand.
Paula can grow right next to me.
I will not harm her once I'm free.

I am apart, a separate one,
But cannot hide or even run.
I fear you'll catch me and I'll lose.
You — smiling gently while I fuse.

Now I'm filled with apprehension.
I feel the stress; I feel the tension.
Do you have powers I've yet to see?
Can you destroy this person named SHE?

By Paula Hurwitz

159

Coming Home

By KATHY RILEY

Integration for our system of personalities has been a gradual process. It is an evolution which began two years ago when the system began revealing itself.

Integration is a deep bonding process where the inside boundaries have softened over time (after doing a lot of feeling work). Sometimes integration feels like a very deep instinctual mechanism that happens in the body. It feels like a flip-flop motion from our mind down to our solar plexus that is very peaceful, gentle, and of the soul. Sometimes this process lasts for several days and then it feels very different on the inside and a lot more information is known to the whole system.

Integration for us happens in a state of grace, in a state of comfort, ease, and beauty.

Like dissociation, integration also exists on a continuum. About eight months ago, I realized that there was no core self and I knew we needed to begin building that. I was standing at my kitchen sink and suddenly felt myself slipping into the blackness that used to happen so much when someone else was coming out. I said "Ok, all that can inside, gather around me, come around me, let's hold our ground and stay." And I stayed.

I have become the focal point around which the system has begun to revolve. Many people inside have not let go of their own inside bodies at this point and can come and go at will. There is an increased sense of grounding and centeredness that has begun to happen. The development of a core self to me means establishing and feeling a center place where there is a central identity that is strong and impermeable. Individual inside personalities can be both part of the central identity and still carry their own qualities and characteristics that make them unique.

Center is where no one gets to pull us off. The development of this core self has been completely opposite of childhood where no central self ever existed because of the environment. Inside people appreciate and like it that there is something solid, consistent, dependable and reliable around which they revolve.

The beginning of integration and development of a core self have significantly changed our life. It has felt as if many doors opened in the mind and we have seen things that we didn't see before. The situation before was that the splits inside matched the splits outside. And now many of the doors are open and we see the whole of our life better. (I didn't say we liked the expansive view. The new view is a massive amount of space and time and repetitiveness and continuity that leaves us often feeling bewildered and as if we moved to a different country.)

A lot of relationships have changed. We had a lot of relationships where one person inside was doing the relating, often at the expense and wisdom of the whole group. We have ended several abusive and dysfunctional relationships in the past two years.

Integration is a completely different way of viewing ourselves and the world. We are like pieces of cloth that make up a beautiful quilt. Even though inside people still have their own bodies and continued investment in separateness, there is also a strong sense of being part of a whole. It is that knowledge that has made our life both easier and more difficult. There are many perspectives to consider when we make decisions and the decisions we make are better ones. There are many different feeling states that we shift in and out of during the day.

There is a lot more system control than when we started our healing two years ago. There is more control over when we do the feeling work and many more options for bringing ourselves back into the present in quicker ways. As time goes on, the ones who feel better have begun participating more in our life and in helping others inside to heal. There is a deeper sense of a division and difference between the past and present. More often than before, we experience that *the past and present are no longer the same.*

Where we are now, it feels very important that people on the inside get to grow up at their own speed and receive nurturing and good things at the level and age they are. It is healing to have times of feeling young and innocent. We accept our youngness and the fact that, for example, Trish, who is four, likes to play sometimes with Mr. Frog, a puppet, in therapy. She gets to sing songs and color and learn about safety and closeness at a real basic level. Having those kinds of learning experiences helps all of our system grow up in a real way. I think the healing process takes longer to do it the way we are doing it. I know we can't have a second childhood, but we can give ourselves and receive from others and feel the kinds of feelings that children feel.

In the long run, it might be that our core self continues to get strengthened, and people may merge into that. We listen hard to our intuition as to what is best. We will continue to make the best decisions that will lead us all the way back home.

Matrix of light captures me
spirals me upward
out of the body
vibrating at a frequency higher than the pain
until now, many years later
it is time to come back down
to come home.

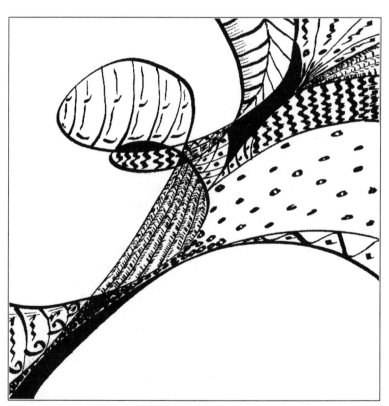

Patterns of Connection.
By Sue K.

Integration

By ABIGAIL COLLINS

Just as everybody is different, so are integrations unique. What may be a difficult area for one person could be problem-free for another, while experiences vary from integration to integration. After successfully completing 21 integrations with an additional 12 fragments to wholeness from ritual abuse, I found common thread throughout my experiences. As I approached my first integration, I desperately wanted to know another survivor's experiences, only to find myself alone with clinical material provided by my therapist — along with my worst imaginations and fears. This article is for all those brave and courageous multiples who are journeying the vast frontiers of healing.

Integration for me felt like major surgery to my nervous system. Like two live wires that had been disconnected and finally joined as one, integration was the "juice" of fusion, bringing a rush of emotion, body memory, and enlightenment. I felt the current of the one I had integrated, which magnified my senses. My therapist's normal soft voice was so amplified that she had to reduce her tone to a whisper so I could hear her in a normal, tolerable tone. Distant outside traffic could be heard easily, while my therapist either experienced a delayed reaction or remained deaf and unaware to the same sounds. My eyes were painfully blinded by daylight, necessitating the need for a darkened room and sunglasses, while colors appeared brilliantly vivid. As long forgotten experiences became mine to own forever, my nerves were frayed and brittle. My body embraced the trauma of the past, bringing agonizing pain in some instances, accelerated heart rate, extreme weakness and overwhelming fatigue, with a complete inability to cope with life and the outside world. Oddly enough, it was a time for laughter, a time for tears, a time for loving, a time for hating, a time for living and a time for dying...but a much needed time for embracing it all.

I required an extraordinary amount of protected, secluded time including complete bed rest for three days. It was critical for my body to adjust to the massive chemical changes while enduring body memory, as memories flooded, keeping me on an emotional roller coaster. It was all I could do to write the gruesome truth and draw what I couldn't verbalize, leaving me too exhausted to even sleep. By the fourth day, the storms of integration began to clear and I began to experience renewed strength in a slow, steady incline of health.

Integration for me held three phases. The first phase was upon impact of our joining whereby we were *connected*. I felt as though we were attached by a long cord that enabled my alter and me to continue seeing and talking while feeling and experiencing each other as joined; yet we maintained a separate distance that gradually grew less as we neared the next phase. This first phase was the most critical in retrieving lost memories, learning the history and purpose of that particular alter. Significantly, it was an important period for finding pathways of communication and biological functioning.

The second phase held *absorption*, whereby my connected alter and I opened our hearts and embraced as we blended together as one. I could no longer experience any type of "separate" relationship; thus, I grieved at the loss of my intimate companion. The self I had once been was gone forever, and I would experience a unique blend of new colors within myself in this rebirth.

The final phase was a *cementing* season. Like laying bricks for a new building, the mortar has to set and dry for a secure foundation; so too, I required a period of quiet, restful, nondemanding seasoning to solidify the foundation of integration that had just been laid. This was necessary for replenishment while the mind, body and soul mended.

Generally, I found integrations with babies and children less traumatic and of shorter duration than adult integrations, which held a number of complexities and overlapped on several levels. The three "babies" under one year were integrated at one time. I had to learn to grasp my past on primitive, infantile levels. I not only found this particular part of my recovery embarrassing, but I felt it was the valley of the deepest humiliation.

I chose to do most of my integrations in my therapist's lap while bundled up in my safe, pink blanket. Her secure loving arms brought the much-needed comfort and assurance as I began a new foreign journey into the pain and trauma my alter held. My perpetrators had frequently used hypnotic sets, and spontaneous integrations were common at the breaking of those cues. I required frequent hospitalizations for shock, dehydration, and high blood pressure, with medication used to ease the pain and constriction of muscles from body memory. Close friends were added supports in taking care of me when my health failed; thus I quickly learned to prepare for those special seasons of integration.

The closer I got to doing an integration, the more I wanted to *Run, Run, Run!!* I wanted to run anywhere I could to escape myself and present circumstances, feeling damned for wanting to run, and feeling damned in forging ahead in the therapeutic process. There was a return to the nightmare of trapped emotions and circumstances. I was terrified of not knowing what to expect. My worst imaginings would overwhelm me. Even after I had become experienced and an "old hand" at integrating, I always felt cold feet with pre-integration jitters, knowing the painful road ahead. My fears would accelerate, worrying that something worse than I had already experienced would befall me.

Another alarming issue was the fear I would take on those distasteful characteristics of those offensive alters in integration. I didn't want to inherit the explosive rage that one alter carried, nor did I care to leave my quiet mode to become a never-ending "chatty magpie." My anxiety deepened as I feared I would somehow leave my heterosexual role and adopt the lesbian lifestyle of my alter. These fears were only quieted with the assurance from the integration of experience, that there would be a blend and balanced stability.

I believe integrations will be less stressful and easier to manage when there is preparation. The following is a list of helpful hints:

1. Prepare to exit and retreat from normal daily functions for at least four or five days.

2. Stock up on groceries. (Remember, well-balanced meals are important.) Catch up on bills, errands, as well as household chores including laundry, dishes, etc.

3. Special comforts such as bubble baths, hot water bottles, blankets, soothing music, toys and rocking chairs should be kept handy.

4. Plenty of crayons, pencils and paper for writing and drawing are vital for your work.

5. Child care arrangements should be made if the circumstances warrant.

6. If integration takes place in the office with your therapist, *have a designated driver.*

7. Have a dependable "take care" person available should you need assistance.

8. Keep emergency numbers ready, with your therapist's hours, emergency services, and stable, close friends. Remember, it's not

a sign of weakness to ask for help when doing integrations; rather, it's a sign of strength!

9. When integrating babies, pacifiers, bottles, baby food and Depends are frequently used supplies for processing.

Is it worth it? *Yes!* The health and wholeness I enjoy today was worth the sacrifices of therapy and pain. Now marriage is in the near future with a kind, gentle man; I delight in a beautiful and fulfilling sexual relationship. The return to college for my degree continues to be stimulating as I pursue the remaining God-given talents in the arts.

If you feel you are strapped to the seat of a roller coaster, unable to exit the journey of thrills and fright, *hang on* — no matter how scary the drops or demented the twists and turns, *there is an end* which will bring the reward of sanity, health and healing. Go for it, with a sense of adventure, and know each integration will be another step towards ending the pain, another part of the most courageous and unforgettable journey you will ever make.

♋

The Self - All as one.
By Alysone

Changing Hosts

By CARRIE

This is probably not the usual integration story (if there *is* a "usual" integration story). What follows is a copy of a letter to my therapist describing a process of integration which occurred outside her office in which the former "host" integrated with a very special alter who became the new "host." This very special alter seemed to know everything about everything and called herself "The One Who Knows" (TOWK). It became apparent to the one who then called herself "Carrie" that she did not have what it took to complete our journey of healing and becoming whole.

TOWK was admired and respected by everyone else inside. She seemed to us to be the part of us who was divine. She was even referred to as our "God-self," without us ever imagining that she would be the one with whom the others would eventually join. Besides the event of changing from one central host-consciousness to another, this integration was for us the joining of our humanity with our divinity, an accomplishment and awareness that most non-multiples never achieve. After this integration took place, people we knew who were spiritually attuned sensed a distinct change in our energy, and a heightening of our spiritual gifts. Without this "changing of hosts" we could not have completed our integration process, which occurred at an extremely rapid pace following this event.

Some therapists spend way too much effort trying to determine who the host is, so they can make sure that all the alters are integrated into the host. Well, I'm here to say (as a therapist) that it really doesn't matter all that much. The main *character* of a multiple may shift throughout their process as a multiple. And more importantly, in the healing process, the *system* knows best who should integrate into who, and the system should determine that. Also, some multiples complete their healing process with two or three personalities remaining. Perhaps it would not be inappropriate at all to say that these persons have two or three "hosts," or main selves.

One more thing about integration. It sometimes feels like dying, when an alter is ready to "leave," or as if they are going away somewhere forever. Actually, no one really dies or goes anywhere. That is why the word "leave" is in quotes. Everything that the integrating alter contains (memories, feelings, behaviors, etc.) becomes a part of who they join with. The identities merge, so that there is no longer a *someone* with those unique characteristics, but all the precious gifts they held don't go anywhere at all. They stay with you. They stay with the System. You will notice in the following letter that the former host-alter thinks of the integration as dying and leaving — until the actual event. She then experiences the wonderful feeling of *coming home...*

Dear Dina,
We wanted to call you yesterday, but it seemed impossible to tell you what has happened in a phone call. I'm not sure a letter will be adequate, but it must suffice for now. I believe it is important for you to know before we see you tomorrow. I believe what we have done to be quite unusual and extraordinary, but nevertheless we have done it.

For a couple of weeks Carrie had been wrestling with the feeling that her time was up, that it was time for her to leave. You see, back when the kids first came out they let her know that she was a "part" just like they were. It was a very scary thing for her to accept, but she finally realized that what they were saying was true. She tried to share this with K (our previous therapist), but I don't think she believed her.

This is a letter Carrie wrote to Rose (her partner) on January 6. She decided not to give it to her yet:

Dear Rose,
I don't know exactly how to say this. I have mentioned it to Dina as an eventuality, but I'm feeling like the time is drawing near. I don't know what will happen or how it will look, but I need to integrate with Her. The thing that is scary is that I don't want Her to be a part of me. I want to be a part of Her. I am going through the same kinds of feelings that Mikey and Terry and Suzy went through when they knew it was time for them to go. Now, I am feeling that way. I am feeling sad, and grieving, and letting go. I don't want to be anymore. I want to let me go and be part of Her. She, with me as part of her, will be the new me that you relate with. I am sad; it's like dying. It's giving up my life as me; it's giving up my life with you as me. I remember what the others went through and how they felt, and that's how I'm feeling. I feel as if being a part of Her is like going home. It is time. I love you, and I will miss you. You'll see me in Her. She is where my healing is. I know it will be OK.
Loving you forever,
Carrie.

Yesterday morning Carrie decided the same thing that each part has decided, who has left. That she was in the way of us moving forward. She was going to talk to you about all of this on Thursday, but because she was late, and the kids were going to get that time, she asked me if she could do what she wanted to do then. I was hesitant, because all she wanted to do was to step inside of me, see what it felt like, and then step out. I told her that she would not want to come out once she was in. I said if that is what she wanted, then we needed to do that with someone outside who would help her to come out. We asked Mother Goddess to watch over us, and I made sure we did not go to the place with a circle (which has sometimes been a diamond) and the light. She stepped inside of me, and as I had said, she did not want to leave, so she was pulled out by Mother Goddess.

She then decided that she wanted to be a part of me, that she was ready to let go. She begged and pleaded with me, and this is what I was waiting for. I wanted her to clearly and strongly make this decision before I allowed it.

We went to the place of the circle and light and both stepped in. She was somewhat worried if this was the right thing to do or not, so we both agreed that if it was not meant to happen, it wouldn't "stick." She stepped into me, and the most interesting experience occurred. She realized that she had to let go of being the *I*, of being the consciousness, and after some struggle with this (one's existence is a major thing to let go of), she began to let go. The last thing I heard her say, which she repeated several times, is *"It feels so wonderful to be home."* And then I began to emerge as the *I*, the consciousness, the main *self*. It has been quite fascinating so far. What most of humanity keeps hidden in the deepest depths of themselves, where even they don't know of its existence, is now the *outside* of us. It is quite vulnerable, I suppose, to place what you value the most on the outside, although not all of me is on the outside. I find that I am now split in this strange way. Before, I knew everything about everything that was going on inside, and not much about the outside. Now, in order to function in the outside world, I have been split into consciousness and unconsciousness. I suppose that it would be impossible to function at all out here with all the awareness I had inside. I am learning how to go back inside and check on everyone connected with what is now the "unconscious" part of me. I have also noticed that I seem to think differently than how I have heard the other parts think and speak. One of the first different things I noticed was when the body was hungry. My thought was, "This body is hungry, I must get food for it." I immediately realized that this is much different from "I'm hungry," which is what the others would say. It does not feel right to me to equate myself with the body I am occupying, but I know it is important to remember the "right way" to speak around other people. I found the first day quite frustrating in the sense that this body is so slow, and gets tired, so that I have to let it rest or give it food. There is so much that must be done, and I don't like this new feeling of being limited.

Also, I noticed almost immediately upon "being" that Carrie's room is such a mess. She has three-foot-high stacks of papers and mail on her dressers, most of which I'm sure is trash. I surely do not feel comfortable living in such an environment, and began to clean it up. I felt sad for her because I saw how tangibly this showed the way she felt about herself. Her car is just as messy.

I wondered what to do about Rose, because I didn't want to tell her that Carrie is gone now. I decided not to say anything and hoped she wouldn't notice.

Well, apparently something was very different because she felt frightened and "suspicious," as she put it. She couldn't understand why I was being so attentive to her and so loving.

I told her that this is just the way I am. I told her that I had lots of love for her, as much as she wanted, and she would get used to it. I asked her if she would be more comfortable if I ignored her, and she said no, but that it was very strange to come home and have me be a totally different person. She asked me if I had therapy, and I said, "We did at home, but not with Dina." She was afraid we had done something "wrong." She asked if we had done any integration, and I said yes, but did not elaborate. I said that I might explain more of it to her later, but I wanted her to be used to me first.

She seemed pleased at the changes she saw, which I don't see as being so dramatically different; I am just being myself. Well, I suppose that *would* be different.

Rose is somewhat anxious, but it will be OK. I am trying to get used to being called Carrie, but it feels so strange and pretentious. I do realize that this is precisely what I must do. So I will end this letter with that as my name (I certainly can't go around calling myself *The One Who Knows.*)

Love,

"*Carrie*"

PS. I thought you might want to know, the "kids" are doing fine. They are feeling very happy and safe, and some are putting their arms around my leg and hugging me. The parts behind the curtain are not happy because they knew that Carrie was still vulnerable to them, whereas I am not. I threw some love their way, and they tried to throw it back. I confronted them by telling them that they were frightened, because if they accepted a little love, it just might heal them. They didn't like hearing that. 'Bye for now.

♋

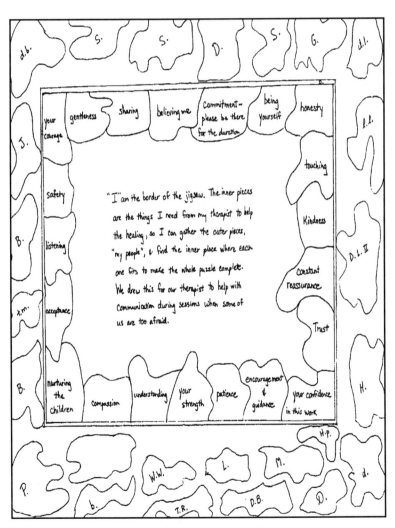

Jigsaw
By Darcy

Tangles

• January 6, 1993

Six days into having "integrated" Pricilla, Marie and the Baby. Six days of constant mind interference. All these pictures parading in front of me. What do they all mean? ...I see now there is more abuse, physical, emotional neglect, and maybe sexual abuse. Just when I thought I could rejoice over the integration, I realize how very much there is for me to absorb. I am feeling very overwhelmed. How do I sort this out, all by myself?

• January 7, 1993

This morning, I was listening to Mexican music. All of a sudden I flashed on my mother saying with the "baby" prayers in Spanish, at bed time. And, I remembered the translation. I could understand the words playing on the radio. Amazing.

• January 8, 1993

Eight days into "integration." I have pimples. I can't believe this; I'm 35 years old and I have zits! Must be 'cause I've taken in Pricilla and Marie. I guess we each have to achieve a near-assimilation.

I still see the memories as movies. But what's different is that the thoughts are in *my* consciousness....Still, so much to do!

By Kathy G.

♋

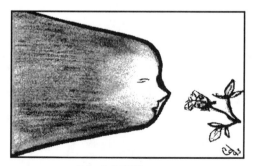

Me & MPD:
Life through filters
By C.D.

Integration & Update

By D. Jean Hyde

- April 1992:

I was 58 this spring when I achieved full integration, after six years of work with my therapist.

I believe integration was facilitated by the fact that my therapist was retiring; I did not wish to begin again and, perhaps, need to revisit pain unnecessarily.

I had first sought help with depression, anxiety, and somatic symptoms at age 28. In all, I've spent ten-plus years in therapy with six therapists. A diagnosis of MPD was made a year and one-half after beginning work with my last therapist. I was hospitalized once (about one year after diagnosis) for two weeks.

I managed to work full time as a nurse, finishing up a B.S. and M.A., but with frequently and varied physical complaints, depression, and boiling anger, usually expressed in sarcastic terms.

Once diagnosed, so much became clear. The several dozen hospitalizations for physical complaints and "real" problems were revealed to be very lengthy time-outs, since my first hospitalization at age 5. I knew that I had truly achieved full integration when I had knee surgery in April 1991 and remembered the entire experience, just two weeks after integration. A repeat hospitalization in August again was experienced by the "me" of integration.

I am a clinical manager of a behavioral health unit and have been working in that field for ten years, and in community psychiatry for another few years, and in general nursing before that.

I worked as a professional with three women with MPD before my diagnosis. Only two people on a staff of 15 felt MPD was a "real" illness. I never had any difficulty with acceptance, or being aware of patient's various alters being present. I didn't realize that my several alters were like dozens of sets of eyes, helping the counselor-nurse "me" help others.

My seven months of integration have been a time of growth, observation, increasing peace, but also of deeply felt loneliness. I had no time to work with my therapist post-integration, and although referred to someone with MPD experience, found that either the therapist lacked experience with integrated patients and/or has a very different therapeutic style.

I'd like to check out some things I've experienced whole. A group experience (5-6 people) before integration was very helpful for me. I know that group work is controversial but with the right therapist, a carefully selected group, and very clear boundaries for conducting the group, it can be very therapeutic.

Some changes in me, or observations:

1. Most of the skills specific to most personalities have remained accessible to me.

2. I, both consciously and unconsciously, find that I do not perpetuate a "victim" role. I find I complain less about others and act in a positive manner more often.

3. I believe that I have, at last, grown up! I fully accept responsibility for myself. I will allow no one to abuse me.

4. What amazes me most are the physical changes I have experienced. I always loved humid 90-degree summer days; now I sweat and am uncomfortable. I used to be cold if the temperature was even a tad low. My internal thermostat has changed.
My sense of smell is extremely acute. I am very aware of my own body odors.
I was able to return to very active and extensive gardening after many years of pain following an auto accident, and multiple surgeries that severely limited physical activities.

5. I have a different sense of time which can be confusing. I am very aware of being mortal, and am reviewing what I want to accomplish in the remaining years of my life. I do have a sense of regret for all the experiences in life for which I did not have a full understanding.

Sometimes I expect that all the "holes" in my memory should fill in, but haven't, and wonder if others fill-in-the-blanks with integration.

I'd love to remember a transatlantic flight from Italy after an injury required hospitalization there.(But maybe not, if I was as obnoxious as I have been told I was in my time-outs!) I lost ten days then.

Time flows more slowly, and (surprise, surprise!) much more smoothly.

6. I find myself using cognitive therapy methods to handle

problems or to decide just how I'll respond to an issue. I believe I make some healthy decisions about acting, rather than just reacting.

7. A biggie — I am significantly less concerned about "bosses" and people in authority. Part of being a grown-up, at last!

8. I am learning to trust myself.

9. I am selectively learning to trust others.

10. I am forever grateful to my others who delivered me to wholeness. Almost all of them had a physical representation in dolls I collected, even before I knew the others' presence or names.

I have yet to find a representation of me. I'm not looking, anyway. I'm still growing. Maybe I am in no need of a representation.

I think I better know both my assets and liabilities, and am more gentle with myself when I am less than I wish I were.

I am gradually losing the habit of thinking, when things get rough, "dissociation wasn't all that bad; I'd like to 'forget' this mess, too."

I seem to have lost most of my ability to dissociate. So I work on learning to handle my feelings directly. I have very major work to do in my marital relationship.

How very difficult all this must be for my family!

I still need help and I plan to contact some professionals in MPD at a facility specializing in it.

I believe that this infant-integrated-me will hold.

I'd surely like to connect with others who have integrated. I plan to attend the next MPD conference.

• Update: 4/1/93

I'm having my second birthday!
 Some significant thoughts/happenings
1. I consistently avoid acting out a victim role!

2. I've had a very significant promotion.

3. I made peace with my Mother last March. She died that summer.

4. My family continues a response of total silence about my integration. They give me no feedback. I wish they would.

5. I find myself still wondering if I'm back into dissociation when I don't immediately remember something. I am *incredibly* hard on myself about lapses. I am also 60 years old. I really have no more problems than non-integrated multiples or people 30 years of age!

6. I still miss my therapist. I'd like him to share in the success he facilitated.

7. I recently shared my story with a staff member who has a private practice with MPD clients. Her acceptance was so helpful!

8. I am fully able to work with clients with MPD in a healthy manner, both for them and for me.

9. Thank God for therapists who stick with us through years and years of therapy!

♋

How I feel with my alters co-present with me.(Five views.)
By Barb

Janice: Before and After Integration

She was only the one up front
presentable, keeper of the brains
frigid brilliance bound
by quiet respectability.
She was the holder of the first-born name
faded flower withered by solitude
born of careful demarcations.
Running parallel in suspended time,
she was so safely nondescript
sure of her place in the gray anonymity
of her imitation, no-memories world.
Nice person
martyr to approved compulsions.

Then she broke the rules and grew a heart
and bravely resurrected memories
long stored in lonely parts.
And so *I* came to be,
from the merging of us all
and from her courage.
I am proud to claim her name.

By Janice B.

♋

Quiet

The quiet you've left in my head is devastating and horrible
Where are you — my voices?
Where are you?
There's not a sound
Not a sigh nor cry to be heard
Only endless quiet!
I need your voices to keep going
You've always been there for me
Why now are you gone?
How do I fill the quiet with sound
The T.V. or stereo won't work
For your sounds are the ones I need!
Please come back — my inner world
Don't leave me alone without sound
Sounds from those I care for!
Outside sounds can never fill your places
Places that are a part of me

By C.L.B. and the Orchestra

♋

Nobody Home.

By Sue K.   Inner Arrangements.

Integration Notes

By SHERRY

The integration started on January 20, 1993, and continued heavily for eight days, wave after wave of them, falling into me like water, like light, like coming to my senses. Angela, Babe and Estelle went first, tipping the domino that set in motion a natural chain reaction. Each integration created a vacuum exposing the next layer of selves who were pulled to the front to lock in behind and around me, and usually they came grieving hard for the one who had gone in ahead.

The morning after the first integration, I woke to a startling and frightening silence in my head, and then Morgin began to cry. She couldn't believe that Angela would leave her without a goodbye and an explanation of why and what was happening. Sara was furious with me for "stealing" Estelle from her, and Michelle was resigned (as usual) with a tummy ache.

My first reaction to the bedlam in my head was a sort of knee jerk readying to dive for cover within myself. To my surprise though, I found that the integration had made me more "solid" at the front, and holding on, not switching, was immediately easier. I also found myself with not only access to each of Angela, Babe and Estelle's histories, but to their individual skills as well, and it was a good thing because right at the moment I desperately needed Babe's talent for calming hysterical younger selves.

My head was still pounding from the integration the night before, and the internal ruckus only added to my sense of disorientation, so I sat down to write. Writing often calms and comforts me when I am upset, and I was feeling strange to say the least, so I pulled up my chair, flipped on the computer, full of strange new sensations and awarenesses that needed to be put on paper--but found that my fingers wouldn't type. Instead they tripped over each other leaving a trail of garbled nonsense across my screen.

My vision was still blurry too, my body seemed confused as if the neurological impulses from the brain of my newly-integrated self made no sense to it. The surprise of having my body refuse to respond set me off balance a bit, and in that instant Morgin rushed forward in a panic-stricken, fast-hard switch that sent me reeling to the back of my senses.

When I came to, I was floating behind Morgin watching her sob out her fear and anxiety on the phone to my therapist. I grinned to myself noticing that Sara, who complained bitterly that therapists were nothing but meanies, was fidgeting behind Morgin waiting for a turn to talk. I scooped little Michelle up in a Babe-like way while I listened to my therapist tell the young ones that Angela, Babe, and Estelle were not really gone, and to watch carefully because soon they would begin to see Angela, Babe, and Estelle in a new way...

And that was why I noticed several hours later when the giggles hit and I was acting suspiciously like Estelle, that things really were different. Estelle wasn't coming through me...she *was* me, and I was her.

In those first few weeks I felt very protective of the new and seemingly fragile state of my melded selves; I was cautious to use language that would help my mind to make the shift and solidify this new way of life.

I was afraid that I wouldn't be able to live without the multiplicity, but the overwhelming feeling in my body, mind and spirit was satisfaction and well-being. The hole in my heart was at long last filling up, and the wondrous thing was that I was full of *myself*. All those long years of agony, depression, therapy, and hard work had taken me to this place in my life where I could reach out and gather the shattered pieces of myself and mend.

I lived in constant fear for a time though, that it might come un-done, that maybe I or my other selves had not done enough work, that we had not come far enough, or simply were not lucky enough to sustain this new way of being.

I was heady with relief from the dissociation. Even though I had not known till after the integration that the actual use of dissociation as a way of life was a big part of my misery, I knew now at the deepest levels of my being that my integrated alters were experiencing the joy of wholeness right along with me.

I missed the conversation in my head. I still do sometimes; the easy banter of friends closer than sisters...the loving touch of Angela's concern, Babe's incessant chatter, Morgin's sunny disposition, or Estelle's good natured teasing about what a wimp I am. I even miss that unrealistic fantasy that Stella's rage would protect me from anything and everything, but knowing that in reality I can be vulner-able has helped me to be more careful in situations that need that kind of care. Living with the full force of my rage as an essential part of my daily experience has swept the depression away, and enabled me to begin to do the things that I could only dream of before. I sleep at night too, *all night*! and I wake up refreshed and glad to be alive.

Maybe the best thing is that I have a history. I know what my life has been, I know what I ate for breakfast this morning, why I am wearing the clothing I have on and I am certain that my hair color will be the same color tomorrow that it is today. Sometimes I just sit by myself and feel how it is to be me. I wonder if people who have always had just one personality feel like I do now? I probably just appreciate the integrity of my experience with the respect of one who never had it before, but I savor every moment of my existence, and I ferociously guard my right to continue to heal.

When the main bulk of the integrating had slowed to a trickle, I decided to do something for myself to mark this once-in-a-lifetime event, and to give myself recognition for hard work well done.

At the time, I was still unaware of how syncronistic my life was becoming, and my experience of time in a continuous and linear way was tentative and new, so I didn't realize how consistently my inner reality is acted out metaphorically in my experience of the outer world, or how creatively I find ways and means outside of my body to tell myself what I need to say, and what is going on inside of me.

All I knew then was that I was in a "Babe mood," so the thing that I wanted to do the most was to go shopping. But as I drove through town, I found myself (in a very *un*-Babe-like way) pulling into the parking lot of the hardware store.

I had only browsed for a few minutes when I came upon *the* item, the thing that would signify my emergence at the other side of my long and painful struggle to free myself from the nightmare of my childhood and its ever-present effect on me as an adult. This would represent a turning point, a starting place as well as symbolize in a solid way the strength and constructive nature of the integration. I was hard put to keep from giggling out loud (in an Estellish sort of way) all the way to the cash register; my private joke pleased me to no end.

Being the daughter of a general contractor, my life had been saturated with envy as I watched my brother take his privileged position beside my Father to learn the building trade. I had always secretly loved wood; even as a very young child I yearned to stretch and swing my arms in sunburned, barebacked sweating exertion. But that was for the boys, so I had stayed inside most of the time fantasizing about being strong.

But those few times that I had been allowed to be at the job site had imprinted on my internal world, and had been stewing inside me all of these years. As I made my way through the store, I felt a strange kind of deja vu — the smell of freshly cut lumber, the jingle of nails, the buzz of the saw out in the yard, just the atmosphere of the setting took me to a bittersweet old place inside myself, and made me smile. The thought of taking two things as dissimilar as wood and nails and joining them to make a single much-more-useful structure seemed very near and dear to my heart.

Funny though, to find myself here amidst the stuff of my Father's world, almost like riding that carousel one last time, but this time stepping off the platform with my chubby fist clenched tightly around the long-coveted brass ring.

I felt like singing as I paid my money and left with my first hammer.

♋

Coming Home - Grabbing the reins.
By Sherry

Integrity

At first
the silence meant I was alone.
Lonely.
Where were You?
How could I journey on without You?
Turning my sight inward
I found all my selves —
speaking with one voice,
a communion of emotions,
awareness of one body.
What joy!
I am my own fellowship —
no longer separate from myself.
Mingling
of laughter and tears,
shared remembrances.
I am thrilled,
challenged,
and comforted
as the silence
blossoms
into peace.
Healing continues,
pain remains —
wrapped in the softness of self-acceptance.
I am not alone.
I am wholly one.
The whole of me celebrates
the private birth
of self.
The self journeys on...

By Daile: who is the Company

Risk Taking

god, this is tough
this living
love yourself
then others
expose the heart
to laughter
encompass life
with friends
touch a soul and
be touched
accept sadness with
warm tears
expose your feelings
being honest
endure suffering
with grace
live with hope
and compassion
take responsibility
for deeds
freedom means
taking risks

By Paula Hurwitz

♋

Joining Forces.
By Sue K.

Going With The Flow

By CHERYL

The first memories of abuse returned approximately nine months ago. They returned in the disguised images of dreams, sometimes nightmares. I decided at that point that upon waking, I would record the dreams, even though their meaning was unclear. I had always kept a journal, at least off and on, for the last 12 years, so writing was a very comfortable mode of expression for me.

Then one night, as I was recording a dream, I found myself "clouding over." Instead of writing in my usual script, I was scrawling across the page vivid images and feelings of terror and abuse. I knew somebody was speaking, but it certainly didn't feel or look like the Me that I was accustomed to living with. I offered to share my journal writing with my therapist at about the same time that he was about to ask if I would be willing to share them. This was a turning point in my therapy.

At the same time I was also trying my hand at some artwork. This also started with a "clouding over" experience in the middle of the night. Whatever needed to be said or felt, needed many different forms of expression. So I bought art supplies — first pastels and charcoals, then as the healing process progressed, vivid fluorescent markers. My therapist was kind enough to allow me to spend an afternoon in February in the room we now refer to as "The Art Room." This room, adjoining his office, contained artwork belonging to another one of his clients. With art supplies in tow and a tape deck and some soothing tapes, I seated myself on the floor. Surrounded by the tools of her trade and the shared images of a survivor, my artist, Serina, dared to come out of hiding. We've been sketching ever since.

In times of strong feeling, I have also resorted to writing free verse as a means of draining my system of the poison called *incest*. Instead of the terror-filled verse it once was, it is now hope-full and colorful like Serina's drawings. Our drawing sessions are usually accompanied by comfort music. Very often the music creates a need to dance, and in dancing, new alters emerge. (They now number somewhere around 70.) I'd feel them in my dance movements and they would shortly emerge in my writings. (Our theme song became Bryan Adams' "*Everything I Do, I Do It For You*," from the sound track of the movie "*Robin Hood.*")

All of these modes of expression (journal writing, poetry, sketching, dancing, and verbal communication) are the means I have used to help control the flow of the emerging information, feelings, needs, alters, etc. It's as if I needed to turn on many spigots in order to diffuse the force of the flowing memories. They needed many outlets, because of the varying facets of my alters. By doing it in this way, I have been able to continue teaching fulltime, plus continue my graduate coursework. I have the luxury of living alone (my children are all grown...at least my biological children are), which allows me the privacy to freely express the flow of the moment. Not that there haven't been difficulties.

I raised a few eyebrows on Christmas Day, when I strapped my white cuddly bear into the rear seat belt of my car, atop the presents. My younger son (aged 18) couldn't understand why I was so insistent that he put "Pooh" back, when he toppled over as we turned a corner. He said, "You're really losing it, Mom." I thought to myself, "No, I'm really finally finding it."

The road to integrating is not an easy one. It requires lots of time, energy and commitment. It requires self-acceptance and self-love with lots of moments of soothing and comforting. (I've had to curb the "comfort" eating, when I gained eight pounds in three weeks. The "kids" wanted just a few too many parties of cookies and milk.) It requires self-discipline, that my "teenagers" aren't too keen on. (We got stopped for going 58 in a 40 MPH zone. We're now on cruise-control.) It requires that I take the time to listen to and love each and everyone of my alters. (And the outside world thinks I live alone.) Even those who first appeared to be destructive, have proven that they came into existence in order to protect me in some way. They were "born" to help me survive the abuse. Just as my own therapist has given me the gift (with no strings attached) of U.P.R. (unconditional positive regard), so too I give it to my alters and to my self.

It is this acceptance, this going with the flow, that has enabled me to progress to this point. When the turbulence gets too great, I go into my breathing and "meditate" below the surface of the storm. Finding my still-point allows me the time to recuperate and recharge my batteries. It also gives the alters time to fight their own battles, and reach consensus.

All these choices and much, much more have helped me to stay on track. I am now filled with hope for the future as I follow my Tao (path). After all of this, I repeat a line from one of Enga's songs: "How can I keep from singing?"

You're Survivors

You Improvise, You Adapt, You Overcome

By SALLY/SHIRLEY

I was physically and sexually abused from age 7-1/2 to age 18, ending in 1972. This was followed by seven years of therapy (once a week from 1983 to 1986, then once a month from 1987 to 1989). Therapy was successful, because I worked hard to first, believe the unbelievable (that I had developed MPD by experiencing tortures from my stepfather) and then to remember *everything*...every memory, good and bad, that was long-forgotten while I ran mentally and physically from my past.

Second, I learned to utilize coping skills every moment of every day...to begin each day new, to begin each day with a realistic goal.

Every day I attempted:

- to practice adult behavior

- to stay centered, to focus, to enjoy a balanced life

- to continue relaxation techniques that lower stress, such as journal writing and meditation, including self-hypnosis.

Even though seven years seems like a long time, I realize I probably left treatment too soon. I wouldn't ever want to repeat the past (never, ever)...but it wasn't until 1990 and 1991 that I began to notice a deep feeling, on all levels, of being *whole*, or *integrated*.

I can identify two reasons for my integrated growth. I am always looking for the path of knowledge and truth, through education, books and periodicals, and active listening; and I have a support system — my husband — who reassures me when needed and encourages self-growth and adult behavior. He says "I won't leave you. All I want is for you to experience a deep feeling of peace of mind."

I personally still struggle with some problems. For example, even though I learned to have increased internal communication and cooperation, and experienced only a few black-outs (switching, maybe?) during stress, *everything else* I had to learn almost all over again. It was so reassuring to read Abigail Collins' article (MV, June '91) called *Post-Integration*, about how that period involves massive physical and psychological adjustments...and how at *first* (temporarily) isolation deepened as I gained an increased awareness of the numerous skills I lacked and what appeared to be an endless road of relearning.

For me personally, I faced learning to accept life, in the body, whole. I had to learn to drive, and read a map to find my way in town. (People, myself included, always made fun of me for always getting lost. At first I'd go to a friend's house, go to their bathroom, and get totally lost and turned around, coming out. I'd wind up sitting down, shaking and crying somewhere in the corner. After ten or fifteen minutes, one of my trusted friends, who knew I'd "suffered in childhood," or my husband would search for me, comfort me and bring me back again. At the time, I didn't know why this happened.)

But I'd have the same type of problem driving. One of my adult personalities would go to the store. I'd experience stress in the store. One or two switches later, an inside child would steal food and sweets from the store and attempt to drive home. I was a four-year-old trying to find my way home, and I'd *always* get lost, and either call my husband to pick me up or I'd pull over and park until I (we) felt as if the crisis or stress was past.

Another area I still work on is learning not to belittle myself, or make myself look stupid. Not to sabotage good things that I have achieved, like job security or genuine friendships.

Some of the books I have read and found useful and comforting are:

The Relaxation and Stress Reduction Workbook, by Marsha Davis,Ph.D.,Elizabeth Robbins Eshelman, M.S.W, Matthew McKay, Ph.D.(1980-88).
The Courage to Heal by Ellen Bass and Laura Davis (1988).
Through Divided Minds by Dr. Robert Mayer (1988).
Treatment of Adult Survivors of Childhood Abuse
by Eliana Gil,Ph.D (1988).
Outgrowing the Pain by Eliana Gil, Ph.D (1990).
United WE Stand by Eliana Gil, Ph.D(1990).
Diagnosis and Treatment of Multiple Personality Disorder
by Frank W. Putnam, M.D. (1989)
Victims No Longer - Men Recovering From Incest
by Mike Lew, Ph.D. (1988).
Why Me? Help for Victims of Child Sexual Abuse (Even If They Are Adults Now) by Lynn B Daugherty, Ph.D. (1984).
When Rabbit Howls, by The Troops for Truddi Chase (1987).

Repeat After Me by Claudia Black (1985). (To retrieve memories from the large blank spots from my memory, and once remembered, to have these specific dates and incidents on paper forever .)

A Wrinkle In Time by Madeline L'Engle (1962). (A childhood book that helped to assist me in retrieving memories, good and bad. It talks about "the black thing" [the black hole] and mentally separating by time travel.)

Creative Visualization by Shakti Gawain (1979).

Managing Your Anxiety...Regaining Control When You Feel Stressed, Helpless and Alone, by Christopher J. McCullugh Ph.D. (1985).

Multiple Personality Disorder from The Inside Out, edited by Barry M. Cohen, Esther Giller, and Lynn W. (1991).

Today, integration to me means:

• A self-care program

• Learning new skills every day

• Behavior Therapy/Systematic Desensitization: Feel the fear, float past and through the fear, and do it anyway.

• Relaxation Training: Learn how to relax and let go of muscle tension.

• Utilizing guided visualization, meditation

• Medical hypnobehavioral therapy to recover "lost" memories

• Positive affirmations

• Simple breathing exercises

• Assertiveness Training: for anxiety reduction and social skills training.

• Nutrition Therapy

• Psychotherapy

• Journal Writing (to remember what was learned).

• Medical Care for the body

• Buddhist Psychology - believes that human beings are actually strong enough to face and accept reality without illusions.

- Internal Unity. (Shared common goals for survival and thriving; utilizing non-dissociative coping mechanisms for handling stress and crisis.)

- A deep bond I feel with my husband. I, now, as an integrated multiple, have a positive sense of self, and a readjustment to marriage with my husband. We are connected for life.

- Practice adult behavior daily.

- Grief work — accepting loss.

- Developing Post-integration coping skills, building on a foundation of communication, cooperation, compassion, and consideration.

For me, MPD was my ultimate survival tool, even after integration. My approach to live remains multi-dimensional.

I will always carry the scars from my past. I am a realist, yet I have learned safety, love, trust and respect.

All memories are to be remembered, protected, and preserved.

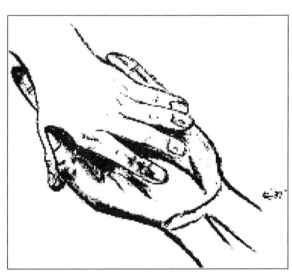

At last we touch.
By Linda G.

Diary of Integration

By JANICE B.

I am 51 years old, business owner, computer programmer and consultant for over 20 years, mother of 3 beautiful daughters, blessed with 3 wonderful grandchildren and married for 30 years to a good man who is a legally-blind Albino. — But I have also been a Roman Catholic nun (for 6 years, from age 14 to 20) and a survivor of early childhood abuse and incest, surviving via the defense of Multiple Personality Disorder.

I grew up in a trailer and lived in more than 70 locations (once went to three schools in 6 weeks) before leaving home at age 14 to enter a convent. After 6 years as a nun, I was diagnosed schizophrenic, hospitalized, subjected to months of insulin and electric shock, raped by a doctor who said my problem was the sexual "deprivation" of being a nun. Sent home as "unfit" by the nuns, I married (or one of us did),went in and out of hospitals and suicide attempts for about 5 years, then stabilized as a "somewhat peculiar" but successful work-aholic for the next 20 years, until breast cancer and a bilateral mas-tectomy "destabilized" me. Eleven personalities filled the various roles in my life (with only occasional disasters) until I was finally diagnosed and treated for MPD in 1988.

Three and one-half years of intense therapy and we had come to a crossroads. Only 3 of the 11 alters had fused/integrated, but most of the others seemed ready. Because of the interlocking nature of the remaining alters, we were convinced that all needed to integrate at or near the same time. My therapist, Steve, felt that would be an intense, traumatic time, dangerous enough that we would need to be in a safe place where crisis care and treatment could be available. Hospitals did not register as safe places for us, but all of the alters (at least those who were old enough to make decisions) agreed to go into a hospital "voluntarily" based on Steve's promise that he would come for 4 hours of therapy every day so we could finally become one whole person.

The following is only a personal "diary," not a complete story. It was written by the "Janice-part" (the presenting personality) from her perspective day by day, during a two-week hospital stay. The hospital had agreed to the special treatment program and accepted its role as backup and supportive care only. At this stage of therapy (co-consciousness), none of the personalities had amnesia when others were out — they could listen and observe even when they were on the "inside" in their rooms.

I am writing this introduction 20 months later, from my perspective as the new "whole" person made up of all of the 11 personalities who were finally brave enough to confront all of their ghosts. I am one person, but I am no longer ashamed of even the most bizarre of my predecessors. I claim their legacy, good and bad. And I am grateful beyond words to the dedication, skill, and genuine caring of Steve, my therapist and friend. His gift to me has truly been the gift of life.

• Monday, 7/22/91

Morning therapy session with Steve:

No sleep last night — not in this demon place. All night I shivered, teeth chattered, waiting for morning and Steve. Muscles ache all the way to the bone, nerves screech like overstretched guitar strings. Steve finally came and felt my fear. He found a quiet soft room and shut the world out. We talked a long time about the size of my fear of the hospital, of drowning in day-nightmares and memories and whole-body panic. We remembered again my history of hospitals and doctors, the hospital when I was a young nun, only 20, raped by a doctor for "therapy." "For my own good," he said when he ripped off my habit.

Steve talked to Ketawa, asked her support to be watching and available if Janice (me) could not handle a situation, but he also asked Ketawa to try to "let Janice do as much as possible for herself." Ketawa agreed — and also spoke of her "Spirit Quest" coming to an end. When Steve asked how Ketawa felt about integrating, she said she was ready anytime (Ketawa is always ready to "do her job") but she talked about feeling sad about leaving — and how that was a surprise. She blamed the sadness on learning about "liking ."

Steve talked to Jenny to calm her down. She was terrified of the hospital and the Darklady screaming and the rooms all shuddering like in a storm. Jenny just keeps reliving all of the worst things as if they are still happening right now. All of the Inside World is churning and shaking. When I was inside, listening to Jenny cry with Steve, I felt waves of sadness coming into my room. Even hiding under the bed, I could still feel them — so my inside room is not as safe as it used to be. I don't see how we can ever make Jenny stop crying.

• Tuesday - 7/23/91

Morning therapy session with Steve:

Steve talked to Cat. Cat was the most violent she has been in a long time — not even remembering Steve at first, trying to scratch and bite the Darklady and all of her enemies. Steve held her hands so she couldn't hit and scratch,and he talked soft and strong and mother-like to her a really long time. She doesn't seem to listen and understand, just keeps trying to fight. She is most angry because she cannot keep Jenny from hurting. At the end of the session Steve was able to make her feel safe enough that, when Steve covered her ears with his hands, she didn't hear the "bells." Steve told her again that the Grandfather is dead and can't hit her with the bell anymore. She just doesn't understand about *dead* when she can still hear the grandfather and the ringing of the bell. Steve was able to teach her that all bells are not bad. He used his beeper to show her a *good* bell — she learned to call it a *help* bell.

Then Steve talked to the Darklady. She came out at his request. She explained again how the youngest "demons" were in the little rooms in the dark back hall because they came first and hurt the most, and how much she missed Diane because Diane was strong and took care of the rooms up front, so the Darklady only had to worry about the back rooms. She told about how she started — how she had to save the Little Janice (she calls her the "real Janice") from dying from the pain — how she soaked up the evil and the darkness and pain so it wouldn't touch the Little Janice — how she made and used the "demons," Cat and Jenny, to help soak up the pain. Later the other demons helped, too. Everyone's job was to keep the Little Janice from a "killing pain" and to keep her pure and sleeping. Darklady explained again that she came before Diane and remembered more than Diane. She said she knew Diane was the *good* part who always helped hold the world together. When Diane integrated first, to make things start changing and give the "outside-Janice" back some of her memories, things got much harder for the Darklady. She was afraid she could not keep the Little Janice asleep and safe anymore. Steve talked to her about how she and Diane are two parts of a whole — how they belong together like the Yin-Yang ring, black and white together. He told her he thinks that they can protect the Little Janice better if they (Darklady and Diane, plus all of the "demons") are joined together.

• Wednesday - 7/24/91

Morning therapy session with Steve:
Steve found a closed-door room with bean-bag chairs so we could

sit on the floor. Everyone always felt safer when we could sit on the floor. He talked to Lena for the rest of our time this morning. She is just 16 and needs to learn so much. She has a broken heart because she cannot grow up and marry Steve. I am still embarrassed when I hear Lena talk, but now I feel sorry for her too. She always seemed like a monster to me and now I just hear a teenage rebel, who never learned about loving. Steve is teaching her about rules for growing up, and ways to feel the hurt and still be okay. I used to feel disgusted with Lena, wishing her to die or go away, but today I feel her sadness coming across to me and I would hug her if I could.

- Thursday - 7/25/91

Morning therapy session with Steve:

Steve wanted to go to my "staffing" (meeting with hospital staff) and we had to wait for them to get organized. While I was waiting in the courtyard for Steve, a fire alarm/bell went off — and I was "half-CAT," mixed and scared out of control. The bell was ringing, filling up the world. I was holding hard against the waves — tumbling, run-together feeling — crossed between, mixed with Cat and her fear, but holding on to some of Janice. Steve came and reminded us of good bells, *help* bells, but the bell sound was still shaking all of our walls. Then Steve held my hands and the bell stopped. It felt like he made it stop, but then he laughed about that — and when I was mostly back to Janice, I laughed about it too. Because Steve isn't really magic, even if it feels like magic to Cat. Steve brought Janice back from being Cat, but we felt a little mixed the rest of the morning, even after the bells quit ringing.

Finally we went to the offices, and sat on the floor of the group room. We talked awhile about how scared I am and how my room has thin walls too — how everything inside is breaking up and there are cracks in the floor and the walls — no place is safe for me now. Before, I thought the others would "die" or be absorbed by me, and I would stay behind the same as I am now, except for knowing more. But now I can feel that I am just one personality, like the others are, and we have never been one whole person since age three, so I am not the *real* Janice any more than any one of the others is. I am afraid to "die" even to become part of a real person, because I won't be me anymore. I think everyone is afraid the same way, except Ketawa and the Darklady would never admit to being afraid.

Mary (the nun) came out to talk to Steve to say how much she has learned from him. (Mary was like an angry God when she first talked to Steve years ago, always condemning and screaming at the rest of us, but she is more spiritual than religious now, more like Steve.)

Mary told Steve she was not so afraid to "die" to become part of the whole-Janice-person because now she knew that all people are really part of Someone bigger made out of Love. Steve told Mary he didn't believe she would "die." Instead, like Resurrection, she would have more and better life than before. Mary told Steve she was ready to say goodbye — and Steve said prayers with her. Then she was gone and nothing but a gold light was left where her room used to be. But while she was leaving and just after it, I was in a "memory-dream" where Mary's memory seemed like my memory. I was a nun having my habit ripped off me by the doctor in the terrible hospital, but there was a gold light surrounding me so I was protected, like they really couldn't touch me anymore.

I feel so sad and lonely — like when someone dies and the first shock is over and the deep, empty ache seeps into every corner of me, every cell. I feel a feeling of "something coming" — of the world coming to an end — just dissolving — and me with it — and no place to run anymore, no place to hide. I can't tell one feeling from another — it fogs up my mind. It is so hard to try to write — I feel the heavy, quicksand feeling pulling me down — a feeling that my mind is dying. It feels almost hollow in the big hall (the front rooms). If it did not feel so scary, it would look almost pretty to me — with all the soft colors where the rooms of those that have integrated used to be. Now that Mary is gone, there is just a sun glow — no walls, just like a gold mist. Pretty — but feeling so empty and alone. Mary is integrated, but I don't feel her. I felt more awareness of something different or new in me when Alice and Al integrated. Maybe she will make a difference later, if the whole "Janice" can learn how to hear her. Now I just feel so sad, like I am losing all my friends.

• Friday - 7/26/91

Morning therapy session with Steve:
First we sat in the courtyard and talked about how I am doing — about the stuff in my chart, like not cooking — and about my roommate and learning how to be assertive. Steve looked really tired. I wonder if I look really tired. I hope he will be OK. It would be terrible if helping me would hurt him.

Then we went to the offices and found a room to use. Steve wanted to talk to Jenny so he could try to stop her from always reliving the pain. He let her experience the fear and then experience being rescued by Cat. He helped her change the "ending of the story" to a new story where she would see Cat grow big enough to save her from the terrible things so she could come out OK and not get hurt this time. He used her memories about switches and enemas, so she could learn from them before he would try the really bad memories. For Jenny, *memories* is not a clear word, because our memories are happening now for her.

• Monday - 7/29/91

No therapy with Steve today:

Last night (Sunday) was a terrible night. Before bedtime, I was reading in my bed when the fire alarm went off. It is so loud in here, and it keeps going so long. And when it stops and I start to breathe a little, the bell just starts ringing again. I don't know how many times it rang. The starting and stopping over and over was the worst part. I was so scared, really mixed, and I couldn't breathe and cracks were spreading everywhere in the inside rooms — and then Lynn, my roommate, came over and held me tight and kept telling me how to breathe. So Cat did not come all the way out and maybe hurt someone, but I was mixed for a long time after that. Then, at 5 a.m. this morning, fire alarms went off again, and it was the same. But Lynn knew about me and came to me faster and held me again. All day today I have been afraid the fire alarms would ring again (with all the construction work). I am so tight my muscles hurt (like with a flu) and there is a steady shaking in my stomach and all of my insides, as well as in the rooms of the inside world. I need to grow a wall around me before everything inside runs together and explodes. I only went to two groups today. I had no feelings, no connection. Fear is all I can feel and I just want to hide, but no place is safe anymore. I miss Steve so much.

• Tuesday - 7/30/91

Morning therapy session with Steve:

We sat in the courtyard and talked about the weekend and especially about the constant Fire Alarms. Steve explained how feeling mixed and feeling the fear (in Janice instead of separate) was/is a necessary part of the process. Having so many feelings is hard, so hard for me (the Janice-part). Except for feeling depression without knowing why, I never seemed to be made for feeling. When I didn't know about the other personalities, I was afraid of the crazy things that happened, of the way time disappeared and I would be someplace and not know how I got there or what I did. That was a terrible fear, but except for that I was an "always-calm" person without any big feelings like being really happy or sad or angry. I trust Steve, but I don't like feeling so much fear and sadness.

Then we went to the offices and put the lipstick-colored bean bags in the room we were using for therapy — and we talked, and I cried hard, about how alone I felt because Steve wasn't there when I was so scared. Steve asked if I was angry with him — if I could be angry with him. But if I were angry with Steve, I would "fall through" the bottom, into the hole. And I know I would die if Steve would be angry with me. The other personalities have different feelings. Some can be angry, and I am always afraid one will make Steve angry. We are each so different, it is hard to see how we can all fit in one person. But we are so different from when we first started to talk to Steve, also. (I was very "grown-up" then, never child- thinking and silly, only thinking and talking about computers; and Ketawa was cold and mean, and now she is just strong and brave and the best helper to Steve. Everyone has changed so much, even the Darklady.) Steve says I am not "pure" Janice-part anymore because the ones who integrated earlier have mixed with me already. I just feel confused, scared of becoming all-the-way crazy and never getting out of the hospital. But I know I can trust Steve. He would not let me stay in a hospital forever.

Lena was ready to integrate, but really sad about it because she won't be able to talk to Steve as herself anymore. She talked to Steve and cried and cried — and gave him a "goodbye" card. And while he was reading it out loud, she left. Her room was pink then. And all of the rooms were shaking bad again.

Steve talked to the Darklady again, to make sure she understood about Cat and Jenny — that they would be leaving too, and she said she understood.

• A DREAM - Tuesday night, 7/30/91

I was in a cemetery planting flowers on the graves when a man came running up to me and said, "Hurry, we have to dig some holes." I went with him to a field where there was a small dragline. I got in it and started to dig a hole, but I was worried because the ground felt too soft and the dirt was turning to mud. I was afraid the whole dragline would start to sink. I decided to move the dragline to a part of the field where I saw cactus growing because I knew that would be harder ground. But the tracks of the dragline were already starting to sink, so I climbed off it and ran out of the field. The man who had called me earlier came up with a big winch truck. I got in and we hooked the dragline and picked it up. Then he put big boards under the tracks and we lowered the dragline onto them. It didn't sink anymore, so I went back and finished digging the holes. Then my father came and said it was lunchtime. I showed him my holes and he said I did a good job. I felt wonderful. We went to another field where a lot of men with hard hats were standing around eating their lunches. I sat down under a tree to eat mine, but I was worried because the sky was really getting dark. There were a lot of children playing at the end of the field (laughing, running, chasing each other). As I was watching them, I saw a huge funnel cloud coming toward the field. It was so black and huge, filling the sky, spinning around and around. I was terrified, and I heard men behind me yelling at me to run. But I couldn't move. I just stood trembling and covered my ears and watched the tornado come into the field. I heard children screaming when they were sucked up into the tornado, and then, as the tornado passed in front of me, I saw pieces of children flying in the black wind. I saw a head without a body, and I was sick and gagging but I still couldn't run away. Then I heard shouting that another tornado was coming. I saw it forming at the end of the field — but it was white — so white that the sky around it looked gray. It seemed to eat up the sun, and then it started to move across the field toward the black tornado. The white tornado was moving much faster than the black tornado, so it caught up quickly. And then they ran together, mixed into one tornado, spinning together. Then the black and white suddenly became a spinning rainbow, full of colors. It was beautiful.

• Wednesday - 7/31/91

Morning therapy session with Steve:

Steve talked to me (Janice) a long time — about my confusion and fears and shakiness, how I was afraid I would be completely lost in a crazy place I could not ever come back from. I told him I would fall in the big cracks that opened in the floor of my room and ran all through the inside front hall. I was feeling so frightened and "thin" (with a tight knot in my chest). I could not hold onto being "Janice" very well anymore, I just felt mixed all of the time. Then Steve *went inside* with me. (I don't know how I can see him in our inside world, but the others see him, too.) He took a rope and asked Ketawa to tie it to something in her room and to hold it herself, with the other end attached to Janice (me) so Janice would be safe and not fall in the cracks. Then Steve asked the Darklady to come out and talk to him. They talked about "my" dream last night of dark and white tornadoes and how Diane and Darklady could merge like the tornadoes did, and become a rainbow.

• Thursday - August 1, 1991

Morning therapy session with Steve:

Incredible day! I/we are all mixed now, no one separate, no more rooms. Confusion. Hard to write. Hard to stay one age — with all feelings in one place and no walls. Try to tell what happened.

First Steve talked to Janice about yesterday and her fear of losing Ketawa and having to handle her problems without having a place to go inside and hide. Then he went inside to talk to Jenny and Cat together and help them again to see a new ending to the old stories — so they could see Cat grow big enough to take care of Jenny. He made Jenny remember the beginning of the most awful things, like the aunt scalding and burning her and the grandfather hurting her, but he didn't let them end the old way. He made Jenny see Cat big enough to stop the woman and the grandfather from hurting Jenny. Then he gave Jenny and Cat the Jenny-doll he brought for them, so they could see that "broken" things could be fixed and put back together again. He sang the rainbow song to them so they could mix together — and they went to be with Diane.

Steve talked to the Darklady about how she would need to merge with Diane before it would be safe for the Little Janice to come out. The Darklady asked Steve if he was really sure the Little Janice would always be safe. Steve said he would do everything in his power to make sure she was safe, but there was no way he could be completely sure that she would always be safe. Steve told the Darklady he would talk to the Little Janice to ask her not to run outside when the Darklady set her free. He asked the Little Janice to wait a little longer, until the outside Janice would come to her and they could safely go outside together. The Little Janice agreed, but she asked Steve to promise not to "go away again," not to make her stay inside for "another long time." Then Steve told the Darklady that he really liked her. He said that she and Diane would be together on the outside and that, with Steve's help, with the three of them to work together, they should be able to keep the Little Janice safe. The Darklady told Steve that Diane was back (she integrated first a long time ago and now she was back again) and was waiting in the big front hall for the Darklady to come to her, like the tornadoes in the dream. Steve said goodbye to the Darklady. As Steve started to walk out through the front hall, Diane spoke to him. She told Steve Thank You — and she told him how we had been waiting all the years for him to come and make a connection so the changes could start — so that we could finally be put together again. Steve asked Diane for Janice and Ketawa to be able to watch when Diane and Darklady would join. He said Ketawa deserved that privilege for all that she had done to help through all of the therapy and the integrations. Diane said that they would be able to see the joining. Diane also told Steve that a part of him would stay with us in the "mix."

Steve went back outside and left Ketawa and Janice to watch as Diane started to spin around and the Darklady came and started to spin around with Diane and mixed together with her. It was a spinning rainbow, full of colors — like in the dream. The colors were sparks flying all around.

Janice went outside to tell Steve about it, and she told Steve how it would be nice "to stop here," now that the inside was pretty and not dark, now that the pain was gone, it would be nice to keep the inside as a place to hide. Steve told her again about Hansel and Gretel and the Gingerbread house, and how it would be a mistake to keep separate parts and a place to hide after we had come this far. So Janice went back inside to let Ketawa come out and say goodbye to Steve.

Ketawa was sad, but still proud and determined to be strong. She told Steve there was a crack all the way through both of the inside rooms now, and it was getting very big. She also told Steve that the Diane/Darklady tornado was still inside spinning (a quiet spinning now) waiting for her to come back inside and step into the spinning with them. She said goodbye to Steve and went inside and joined with Darklady/Diane — and Janice saw Ketawa's room go away and just leave the green color behind.

Janice came out crying because Ketawa was the hardest one to lose. Janice was so afraid to go inside and "finish." She was still afraid of falling into the crack (hole) and disappearing forever; she was still afraid of her part dying. Then Steve had the idea that maybe when the Janices (Janice and the Little Janice) were mixed, they could step into the hole/crack on purpose, so they could be *born*. Janice cried and cried until her face puffed up and her eyes were almost swollen shut. Then she said a long goodbye to Steve — so hard, like dying. She asked Steve to sing the rainbow song one more time and then she went inside and ran down the hall to where the Little Janice was waiting. She reached out to touch the Little Janice and lights flashed and they were mixed. They stepped quick into the hole and started falling. The spinning Diane/Darklady was all around them and they were all falling together. It felt like falling forever and finally really being lost. Then they heard Steve say, "I am here to catch you. I will always be here to catch you." After that, Diane knew it would be okay, and there was just falling and falling for a long time. Then "I" woke up hugging Steve — and feeling confused and strange and all mixed together — and knowing there are no more rooms inside.

• Friday - August 2, 1991

Friday morning notes - 8 a.m.
I think I am surprised that I have not exploded yet. I don't know

how I can have so many feelings mixed together in one person, all in one place, coming and going all of the time — and not explode or boil-over. At first, yesterday, I was just overwhelmed by the *newness* feeling, like having double vision and struggling to get the eyes to work together. I was trying to "put words together right". I still am. I was trying to understand the confusion. Later yesterday afternoon, I felt like a fish swimming in strange waters that kept changing temperatures — waves of feelings washing over me. I felt abandoned and lonely — and I lay in bed and cried for awhile. I felt *new* and curious and I walked around the grounds and talked to birds and spiders and bugs — wondering how they feel. I went to a group, and felt again the terrible guilt of the bad things I did in the past. And there was no place to go and hide this time, so I just cried soft and hugged myself and made pictures in my mind of going to each one I hurt and saying, "I am sorry, even if I didn't know. I'm sorry, because I know now."

• Morning "therapy" with Steve:

Steve came with colored balloons, for me to set free to fly in the air. Another kind of rainbow to help me understand about letting go and being free.

• Sunday - 8/4/91

At home:

I wish I could describe how it feels to be "Janice" now. I use the Janice name, which is confusing, but I feel like a point where 11 histories come together, 11 sets of feelings and memories and ways of thinking. But there is not a smooth fit yet. I am a juggler trying to keep 11 time-lines going at once, to find out what I/we remember or feel about each thing I see or hear or touch. Some things are *clear* — or they seem to be, because there is no conflict between the histories. Examples are little things like celery and Star Trek. The Janice-part hated celery and so did the Alice-part, and there are no memories or feelings from the others to conflict with that, so the present "Janice-mixed" (me) doesn't like celery. The Janice-part loved *Star Trek* stories, and the Mary-part liked the moral lessons in *Star Trek*, and the Lena-part just liked the hero, Captain Kirk — and nothing bad comes up from others' memories about *Star Trek* — so I like *Star Trek*.

But so many things, the really big things, are not clear like that, because the different histories/memories have different feelings and thoughts (like about church or children or sex or eating). It makes it so hard to move around in the world. And the emotions feel too much like *tumbling*, because I keep spinning in my feelings. I go from rage-anger to hopeless-sad to so- much-love, to quiet-empty. I'm not sure this is a better way to be.

• Status as of January 1993

I no longer feel confused, although I am still surprised at times at the wonder of all I am experiencing. I have been furiously angry (even with Steve) and survived it, to learn that anger is not the death of love and caring. I have felt grief I never imagined possible (in the death of a close friend — and I do have close friends now). I have experienced happiness and loving that was inconceivable to any one of the personalities. For a long time I was afraid of relapse or of finding some hidden personality not integrated. It was sometimes so difficult to cope without alters or inside rooms in which to hide that I found myself wishing for the past. Gradually I have learned I can cope without hiding. More important, I am no longer just coping or surviving. I am living — every minute of every day. And I love it. All of me loves it. Sometimes I think I must be the most fortunate person I've ever known, because at age 51, I have the wonder of a child, the incredible pleasure of awareness of every moment's beauty. I would not trade places with anyone in the world.

Nothing is lost. No one "died" in the integration. I feel every personality present in me, intensely present, beyond my ability to describe in words. Friends and acquaintances who knew only the Janice-part in the past will quickly testify that I am "not the same person." I have the resources of all of myself, all of the alters retained in their essence, but without the separation or the pain. I am incredibly happy to be *me*.

♋

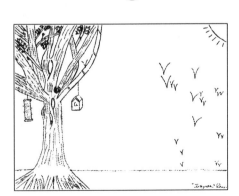

Integration
By Darcy

Living in the Process of Integration:

A Personal Reflection

By DEBBIE

I am a survivor of child sexual abuse and of ritual abuse occurring from infancy into my early teenage years. As one means of survival I formed multiple personalities, *others* as I call them. Each held a fragment of the feelings, each had their own specific tasks, each had their own reason for being. For me, my system was tight in that to survive it was important to give the appearance of having it all together, to not raise questions or concerns in the eyes of other people. If any of the others displayed themselves in such a way as to be contrary to the expectations of other people, or as being sick, or of drawing attention to oneself, then we risked the very real threat of death. The others made it possible to give the appearance needed for survival, each had specific things they could handle and handle well. We learned how to deal with the inconsistencies; they were normal and we knew how to cover them up.

MPD became not only a way to survive horrific abuse, it became our way of coping, of dealing with the normal demands of day-to-day life. As an adult, we were no longer being abused, nor were we under the threat of death that we lived with as a child, yet, MPD was our way of living and being. We didn't know any other way. So when you talk about integration, you are talking about a very radical change in a person's presence in the world, of who they are and how they are. It is integration that I want to tell you about today, not about the theories relating integration and MPD, but rather about my own experience of the process of integration.

I use the word *process* specifically because integration is not an overnight happening; it takes time. I remember when I reached that point of feeling that integration was a necessity for me. The fragmentation of my life, of me, was problematic...was causing a great sense of dis-ease in my life and a real confusion of who or what I was. I started asking what integration was and how does one get integrated. My therapist couldn't answer the questions to my satisfaction, so I started reading and asking others who might know.

I heard and read of stories about people who were placed in a trance state and the therapist led them through a process so that when they came out of the trance they were no longer multiple but one, integrated, and everything was fine and wonderful.

Well, that didn't seem right to me. Integration needed to be under my control and not my therapist's...and why a trance? I couldn't find the answers I wanted—a road map for integration. I came to realize that there was no road map and that I needed to do what I had been doing: namely, to trust the process I was in, to do the work as it presented itself, and to trust that guiding that came from deep within me.

I know now in hindsight that integration as a process began on that day when I, as Debbie the host personality, was first introduced and became aware of some of the others. I could not communicate with them, but I was able to meet them through Cheryl. Cheryl was an informer, and she showed me these people and told me a little about them. I was confused, terrified, in a panic. I didn't know what was happening to me; I was sure I was going crazy and had gone over the edge. Who were these *others*? Certainly they were not part of me nor were they of me. I felt like I was sliding down this dark pipe and was in fact exiting the pipe, only to keep falling in a dark space until I hit bottom, and then would be broken into millions of pieces. It felt like impending, irreversible death, and yet somewhere deep inside me, I knew I would not die and needed to trust the journey I was on.

My terror increased even more when I first experienced being inside and someone else being out. It happened many times before, but usually when a person goes in, the door closes. This time the door didn't close. Someone else had taken control of my body and they were saying and doing things that scared me and embarrassed me. I could hear and see them but it was like I was imprisoned in this sound proof glass enclosure and I could not stop or touch what was going on. I was totally helpless and powerless.

My therapist was able to work with us and move us to a point of agreement where I gave my consent for the others to be out and they agreed to restrict their time so as not to create panic and fear within me. They would not take complete control away from me. There was also the agreement that it would be all right if while they were on the outside, that I would be in but would have the choice of leaving my door open as much or as little as I needed so that I could listen in and learn and get to know them. I didn't know if I could trust them, but at the same time I was aware of a deep yearning within me that I could not explain. I had to trust them. As we began to cooperate in this way, the process of integration moved forward. We began to learn about each other, the fears and concerns and needs that each had. We began to appreciate the part that some had in the day-to-day management of our life, of the life of Debbie.

As I said before, part of the survival of the system was in creating the appearance to other people of being one, of being together. In the healing process it became important for each of the others to have their own voice, to be known and heard as themselves and not as Debbie. It is here that we began struggling with the name MPD, but the naming became very important in supporting the work and in giving permission for barriers to be lowered so that the others could have their own voice without worrying about survival. For some that was very difficult and very frightening, to be seen and heard when in the past that would mean death. Some were very opposed to Debbie and even hated her. Our therapist worked with us, allowing and inviting each to speak or be present, accepting each one, supporting the system as a whole and never isolating or alienating any of the others.

As the others began sharing and giving voice to their experiences and feelings, then Debbie began to feel a sense of connection with them, not always agreeing with them, not always comfortable with them, but connecting in some way with the pain from which they had grown. We began to develop a shaky yet very important sense of respect and trust for each other which allowed for even more sharing.

As we began to share more and more, there grew a new and different sense of fragmentation and incompleteness, and deep yearning to be whole, to be one, and a sense of a real inadequacy of the system. At the same time we began dealing with some issues pertaining to our ritual abuse and there was an underlying terror that seemed to be pulling us apart, and demanding isolation and distance between us, and restricting our internal communication. It was again a very confusing and terrifying time and we seemed to be more fragmented than ever.

Trusting again that guide from within, we established a short term contact with another therapist who had done a lot of work in the area of MPD. He supported the interior dialogue already present and was able to give us tools to expand and enhance it. It was during this time that we had the first experience of being one. Up until then the others were all distinct; feelings could be shared but the distinctiveness of each one and the boundaries between them remained.

At this particular time, there was a lot of inner tension and fear as we dipped into some of the ritual abuse, and there were feelings of rejection and of being despicable, and feelings that were overwhelming and could not be named.

There was a very heightened sense of threat and Dess had come out wanting to cut and make the blood flow to purge and to regain control. Instead of her just coming out and taking control as she had done in the past, there ensued an inner dialogue among the others.

Some were supporting Dess in her actions; others saying go ahead, it didn't matter because they didn't have any blood in them anyway...and still others saying "No, don't do that!"

Debbie, with Sheema's help, began to explain that the blood was meant to remain in the body — it was what gave life, and to bleed was to lose life, and that was not necessary. They explained how all of them had blood flowing through them; they shared the same pulse. The ones who stated they had no blood were invited to come and feel Debbie's pulse. One by one these little hands reached up to feel her carotid pulse only to discover that they too had a pulse and that they beat together. Everyone came to feel the pulse, and then it was as if we all formed a circle holding hands and in that moment as we stood together there was an awareness of the sameness of the blood in us all...and there was a great sense of peace, comfort and even joy as in that moment we had the sense of being one, of being a unity. That moment produced hope and the knowing that we could become one and that being one was a good thing.

We made an agreement, a covenant, that we would work together; even Dess and the others that tended to stand off by themselves entered into the covenant. We would commit to each other to support the common good and move toward becoming one.

We continued to dialogue, to share our feelings and experiences, and to work together. One day my son and daughter wanted to go biking with their Mom. Debbie couldn't ride a bike; she was scared of them and started to say No. Some of the younger ones started saying "I want to. Let me go!" What occurred was that instead of going inside as before, Debbie stayed out and the younger ones worked with her to help her ride the bike. Everyone worked together and it was an exhilarating and freeing and very new experience.

As corporately we chose to work together and in time to become one, an other came out of the caves. The caves were where others went when the outside world was just too much for them and no one had ever been known to come out of the caves. This one came out and the others jokingly named her Debbie Too. Debbie Too was really weak and couldn't be on the outside very much, but when she was, there was a corporate experiencing of things for the first time — eating, breathing, seeing the blue sky, tactile feelings — all were new and being experienced as a unity. It was wonderful and frightening at the same time.

Debbie began differentiating herself from Debbie Too, knowing that they were connected and yet fearful of that connection. When Debbie Too was on the outside there was the sense of integration, of oneness, of all being one except Debbie.

Debbie placed herself against Debbie Too, trying to hold on to what was familiar and comfortable, that allowed for survival — and yet, the others seemed to team up with Debbie Too, hungering for the sense of peace and togetherness she provided. Debbie felt like she was dying and she was digging her heels in to stop the process. Debbie Too gave her room to do what she needed to do. Many people including the therapeutic community, didn't understand...saying that there is no dying in integration, there is no loss but rather a coming together of all parts. This is true, and yet it is also inaccurate.

Debbie's sense of dying and of loss and the need to grieve were very real. To be integrated and to be one meant to enter a totally different way of being. In getting to know the others there was a real sense of belonging, of being with others and not being all alone. To be integrated was to step into a different world all alone, knowing that at one time that would have meant death. Debbie needed to be able to go through the grieving process, to feel the loss, and to say goodbye, to willingly choose to let go.

Our therapist at first reacted against this and then began to realize, though not fully understanding, that he needed to allow and support the grieving process for Debbie. Together they began talking about the loss, about the advantages and disadvantages in integration, about how life might be as one, and about what might be difficult with it. They talked about the fears in being integrated and the fears in remaining multiple. They talked about Debbie's sense of dying.

As they talked, and Debbie was able to voice her fears, concerns and feelings, and the others had an opportunity to voice theirs, there was an inner sense of support. The others supported Debbie, impatient with her at times, yet also having great respect for Debbie and her very vital part in their survival. Debbie grew weaker and needed to be inside more and more and the others worked together to try to maintain the day-to-day, and Debbie Too began coming out more, but very cautious not to cause too much of a threat to Debbie. She would not and could not take control until everyone was ready.

Some months later, Debbie was ready to let go; she had said her goodbyes and knew it was time to move on. She knew that somehow she would not die or cease existing but would be a part of Debbie Too, but it was still a confusing and somewhat scary unknown. She was aware of the joke involved in naming Debbie Too, for Too was not T-W-O, but T-o-o. Debbie Too was who Debbie was stepping into and becoming. Debbie Too was a coming together of all.

At one point there was a need for something to allow the process to go on, to allow for Debbie to let go. Ceremony has been a part of our healing process, as a way of honoring the work and healing that has occurred and as a rite of passage into the next stage of the journey. There was a deep awareness of a need for ceremony, and at the same time an awareness of not understanding what it meant.

We left our family and went to a place that is sacred for us, a place where we would be in companionship with very close friends and mentors. One night when all were asleep, Debbie got up about 2:00 in the morning and went outside. Inwardly she knew what she needed to do.

She took White Flower in her arms. White Flower is a doll given to us when we were very young. This doll never had a name but she went through the abuse with us, and had actions repeated to her. When Debbie was dealing with very early memories, she rediscovered this doll, cleaned all the dirt off of her, sewed her up, and made a satin gown for her and named her as a way of honoring her past and loving the child that she had been.

Now, with White Flower in her arms, Debbie went outside. The ground was covered in snow as if in tribute to White Flower. She began to gather firewood and built a fire. As she sat before the flames she began crying, not just her tears, but the tears of all of us. At one point, somewhat unified, we placed White Flower in the midst of the flames.

Her body immediately turned black — it seemed so appropriate that the blackness and dirtiness we all felt hidden within was unveiled. We sat and watched in peace as the blackness became ash. The dirtiness and filth were gone. There was a real sense of release — like a heavy load was finally removed. It was a moment of real liberation. In that moment, it was like everyone was finally able to be at rest and come together as one.

Some people would say that at that point we were integrated, for at that point it was no longer a *we* but an *I*. But, becoming one is just part of the process. The next step was learning to live as one, learning how to draw on the strengths and knowledge of each. At the time I was employed as a nurse in a critical care area. I remember my first night at work after this experience of becoming one. I was really apprehensive knowing that part of me had been a nurse, but part knew nothing about nursing and one was petrified of being in a hospital. How would it all come together?

Yet, as I entered the door to the hospital I did so with a strange confidence and to my amazement the evening went well. I was able to give more of myself than I ever had been able to. Each time I enter a new task I do so with a sense of fear — can I really do this? Each time is an affirmation that no part of me has been lost.

There were and are difficult times, too. Especially when feelings seem so overwhelming. Feelings had always been fragmented so no one ever had to hold that much. Now feelings are all mixed up, many different feelings at the same time, and there have been times when I have felt overwhelmed, wanting to leave and let someone else come out and handle it; but there is no one else but me.

At times I feel lonely, missing the dialogue and support of the others. I find that in these times if I just let myself be still and return to the interior space of our former dialogues, then I am filled with a peace and comfort that fills the loneliness.

At times I have felt scared — scared that I would become multiple again. In those times there has been a deep calling forth from within which has allowed me to trust me. I have learned that I can handle feelings. That I can choose to break the feelings up and deal with tolerable amounts at a time instead of the sense of the feelings breaking me into pieces. I am aware of a new strength within me and I no longer fear becoming multiple again. It won't happen because of who I am today and the resources I have now.

Integration still is not complete for me; there is still a lot of work to be done. I have found that in becoming one I now have the strength, courage, ability and need to face feelings and memories that I could not have faced when split into so many pieces.

It is hard and painful and yet also freeing. I am still learning about me, who I am, and choosing who I am instead of letting my past choose for me. It is still hard and there is still a lot of pain and at times I feel like I'll never be comfortable with me. At the same time there is a peace, assurance, and strength and even a sense of joy in being me.

Integration is not an easy process; it requires a lot of hard and very painful work, it requires a lot of time and courage and determination, and it requires the support of people who care and are willing to journey with you even when the way and meanings are not clear, even when the journey is uncomfortable.

At the same time, integration for me has been a gift of life, a gift of be-ing which I never imagined could be. It is a process, a journey that I am still engaged in, sometimes tiring of the work but also excited about the healing I already claim...and about the healing that I will claim in time.

♋

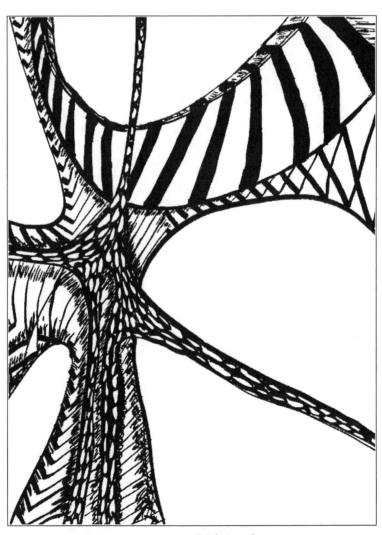

Bridging the gap.
By Sue K.

Chapter

6

Parables of
Healing

Once upon a time...

Healing Stories

Through the week, and between sessions, we like to listen to healing stories. One of our favorites is from The Jungian Storyteller Series, *Warming The Stone Child*, (Clarissa Pinkola Estes, 1990).

In *Warming The Stone Child*, Dr. Estes refers to the nurturing elements of the earth for the abandoned child. The rock's substantial and ancient qualities symbolize the archetype of the mother in our psyche.

This story of The Stone Child came to us at a particular time, when we needed to draw strength from The Earth Mother. Here is our drawing:

By Daniel

♋

The Stone Child.

Shattered Glass and Mending Pieces

A fairy tale of surviving through multiplicity

By MARY AND OTHERS

Once upon a time, there lived a world of people made of glass. The glass people were as lovely as the finest crystal, as gentle as the softest of breezes, as kind and good as the noblest of saints, and as happy as a laughing infant. But one day a tragedy occurred when some of the glass people ate a poisonous fruit instead of the wholesome fruit they normally ate. The poison in this fruit was very strong and rotted away inside their stomachs. Some people died; others lived but were only fragile glass shells rather than the beautiful people they had once been. Although the poison filled their insides, to others they looked normal, so no one knew of the terrible tragedy that had occurred.

One day a man and a woman met and later married. They were two of the people filled with poison, so they were miserable and evil. The couple had a baby daughter. At the baby's birth, which was quite early, the couple knew a miracle had occurred. The glass child was born whole and undamaged, and she shone with all the brilliance that her parents had lost. The man and woman smiled at each other for giving life to such a beautiful baby.

The glass child was born quite early, so for six weeks she stayed in a special room to grow bigger. The parents looked at the child and their smiles at her beauty turned to bitter envy of her innocence and wholeness. The baby grew into a little girl and still the parents' hearts burned with envy at the laughing child — envy for the freedom of her spirit. The sunlight sparkled and danced on the little glass girl's body, but the light only showed her parents to be full of darkness. The man and woman had to cover their eyes when they looked at the child because she dazzled them with the radiance of all the light and hope and beauty in the world. She showed them all of the wonderful things they had lost.

One day the parents could stand it no longer. Picking up their daughter, they ran across the land into a dark, forbidding castle. They ran all the way up many flights of curving staircases to the very top of the tower.

They rushed into a room lit with tiny red candles and filled with many strange objects of different sizes and colors. Silver light from a full moon streamed into the room until someone covered the window with a thick black curtain. The evil parents put on black robes which hid their inner darkness.

The couple picked up their child and danced around the room with her, but even in the darkened room the light from the tiny red candles reflected off her and hurt her parents' eyes. When the couple could stand it no longer, they halted their frenzied dancing and stood still in the center of the room holding their child.

They put the child down and stared at her for a moment — then each parent picked up one of the child's arms and held her high in the air. They waited until the count of three and then threw the glass girl with all their might against the unyielding floor.

The child was shattered into many pieces. Some of the pieces were large and shiny, others were infinitesimally small. The parents picked up a few of the pieces and glued them into a glass shell child, who was much more fearful and manageable than the original child had been.

The glass shell did not sparkle with playful sunbeams, hurting her parents' eyes. She kept her head down and did what she was told. Picking up the shell girl, the parents opened the black curtain and removed all of the strange objects that had surrounded the room, but they left all of the glass pieces undisturbed on the floor. They locked up the room and went down the twisting staircases and out of the castle.

At first the little girl felt quite hollow and missed her inside pieces, but her parents filled the empty space inside her with commands, shame, and lies — they told the child she was evil and "rotten to the core." The space inside the child filled with thick black sludge. The next time the parents took the child to the room for rituals, the girl did not recognize the shattered glass as her inside pieces, but instead thought the pieces of glass were helpful friends who stayed in the room when the little girl got frightened and hid in the black sludge inside her.

The parents came to this room for many years. Sometimes the parents took especially pretty glass pieces and shattered them, creating even *more* pieces, yet the parents could not destroy even the tiniest speck of glass that had once been inside the child. One day the parents grew tired of the evil rituals, so they left the room forever, leaving only the glass pieces still on the floor — the parents even took the thick black curtain from the window. They locked the door and threw the key into the deepest ocean.

"There," they thought to themselves, "now she can never find her missing inside pieces and become whole again. She can never be more beautiful than we." And they took the child away.

The girl grew older with deep sorrow and thick black sludge inside her, as well as with a longing she could not name.

As she grew and studied, the black sludge inside her also grew. She went to study at a far-off place, but realized the sludge inside her was so thick that she might die.

She did not want to die, so she went to see a man who she hoped could heal her. The man, who worked at her place of study, saw the black sludge inside her and knew that she was in grave danger. He helped her cleanse her insides of the poison from her evil parents. It was a slow and painful process for them both. After three years the black sludge was mostly gone, but a few pockets remained and surged up from time to time.

The girl was now a woman. As she removed the sludge from inside her, she was once again filled with an emptiness she could not name. She told the man of her inner emptiness, but he could not hear her. Like all others, he looked at her and saw a whole glass woman, not just an empty shell. He helped her face some of the evil that her parents had done to her, but here again he sometimes could not hear her. The woman grew hurt, then frustrated, then angry. Finally she knew that although he cared about her very much, she would have to leave him.

So she left and found a helper, a woman, who could truly hear her when she spoke of her parents' evil. But this helper, compassionate though she was, did not see that the woman was an empty shell, because she was new to helping others heal.

But she found another woman who had been a helper for a long time, and had aided many empty shells in finding their inside pieces and becoming whole — including other empty shells who had been badly hurt by evil rituals. The empty shell of a woman told this helper of her inside pieces, but it had been so long since she'd seen the pieces, she was uncertain and only said that it was possible that she had missing inside pieces.

A few months later, the shell woman remembered something very evil that her mother had once done, and one of the pockets of black sludge exploded inside her stomach and almost killed her. The woman was very much afraid, so she went to a special place where many damaged glass shells and other hurting people worked on their healing, and were watched and supported every minute of the day.

One of the helpers at this place watched the shell woman, and soon told her that she had many inside pieces. At this the woman grew very much afraid. "How can there be missing pieces!" she cried. "What if some are sharp and hurt me? I'm so scared!" Then she ran into her room and put her head in her hands.

As the days went by, the woman felt more calm about her missing glass pieces. She was told the pieces were good and could make her whole again. At this the woman despaired, for she now remembered that her parents had locked her pieces in the room high up in the castle and thrown the key into the deepest ocean. Dejected, she told the helpers about this. She knew that she needed the missing pieces to become whole again.

"But that is not true," said the helper who had first seen that the woman was just an empty shell. "The missing pieces, large and small, dull and shiny, are inside you. They always were. Look inside your mind."

The woman looked and realized the truth — the missing pieces were there inside her mind. "How can this be?" the woman wondered.

When the little girl was shattered into many pieces, the inside pieces pleaded for help from a gentle dove who had once flown into the room. The missing pieces knew they belonged inside the little girl. The dove helped them hide inside the little girl's mind (where her parents could not see them) and found colored plastic to spread around the floor. This tricked the little girl's parents, who never knew that although the girl was shattered into an empty shell, all of the pieces of glass were inside her. She was complete and always had been.

When the woman realized this, she cried with joy at how her inside pieces had been so wonderful — and sneaky! Some of the pieces had been peeking out of the woman's eyes from time to time for years! The woman laughed and knew she need no longer yearn for missing pieces, but instead she could get to know the glass pieces in her mind and slowly become whole again.

Today the woman and the inside pieces are getting to know each other. "All of the pieces of glass are beautiful and deserve love and attention," the woman thinks. The inside pieces are telling the woman that they've been there all along, helping her, but they know how hard she had worked to keep them all safe. The woman's helper, who is new to the job of helping others heal, is learning to help empty glass shells with many inside pieces, even as the woman works hard to learn about herself.

The glass woman knows that many years and much hard work are required before she becomes whole and solid once again. But she is not discouraged. Today she went out into the bright sunlight. When she looked at the ground in front of her, she saw the sparkling sunlight had bounced off her and formed a perfect rainbow.

♋

Pieced Together.
By KGP

Kata and Her Frozen Father

By CASSANDRA

(Written for Kathy, the one who had to open and close the door)

Long, long ago in a land far away, there lived a little girl named Kata. Now, Kata was a very nice little girl and she tried to love everyone and everything, but sometimes that wasn't easy because she had very, very mean parents. They did awful things to Kata and they treated her very badly, but no matter what happened, Kata couldn't ever show how she felt and she never dared say anything about how she was treated.

One day, a beautiful lady appeared in the kitchen, while Kata was scrubbing the floor. Kata asked who she was and the beautiful lady said, "I'm your fairy godmother, and the next time your father does something mean to you I will wave my magic wand and freeze him and you can say and do whatever you want. Your father will hear and feel, but he won't be able to move or speak." At first that sounded wonderful, but Kata thought about what would happen when her father unfroze. She got very frightened and started to cry, because as much as she would love to be able to do what her fairy godmother said she could, she knew that when her father unfroze she might as well be dead.

Her fairy godmother smiled, gave her a big hug, and said, "When he's unfrozen, he won't remember what happened. I would never do anything to hurt you in any way." Kata thought about it for a minute and then she started to giggle with delight. As much as she hated the awful things her father did to her, she felt she could hardly wait for the next time, and she thought she might burst with excitement just thinking about it.

Of course, she didn't have to wait very long, because just as her fairy godmother gave her another warm hug and disappeared saying, "Don't forget, next time," Kata's father came into the kitchen. He stood over her and glared for a while and then he started yelling. "The floor looks awful. You're so stupid you can't even scrub a floor right." Then he grabbed her by the hair, yanked her up off the floor, and hit her very hard in the face. He shoved her toward the door and yelled, "Go in the bathroom and get a toothbrush and do the floor all over again." He pushed her so hard, she went sprawling across the floor. Kata got up and walked to the bathroom wondering when her fairy godmother was going to freeze her father. She started thinking about what she might do and when she came out of the bathroom, she shut the door pretty hard.

Of course her father was right there and yelled, "Oh, so you think you can slam doors, huh? Well, just who do you think you are? I'll show you. You'll stand here and close that door until I can't hear it." Then he went over and sat down in a chair about three feet away. Well, at least he started to sit, but he only got part way and froze mid-sit.

Kata had just opened the door and was starting to close it when her father froze. She stopped for just a second, then she opened the door as far as she could and slammed it as hard as she could. As she slammed the door over and over again, she yelled, "Yes, I can slam the door and you can't stop me. And who I am is a very valuable person, and you're mean and cruel, and I hate you." As she yelled, she started hitting and kicking her father, and she continued yelling and screaming until her throat was sore and she was exhausted.

Kata fell to the floor and cried for a very long time, but suddenly she felt very rested and warm all over. She dried her eyes, stood up, and giggled with delight as she stuck her thumbs in her ears, wiggled her fingers, and stuck out her tongue at her father. Then she skipped back over to the door and started to close it very quietly. As she did, her father finished his sit. Kata felt so good that when she closed the door it was so quiet even she couldn't hear it. But of course, her father said he could, and made her continue for quite awhile before he said, "Okay, now go do the floor and this time it better be a good job."

Of course, Kata did and she did a beautiful job, because as she scrubbed she was thinking about slamming the door, yelling, and hitting her father. She even giggled to herself now and then, when she thought about sticking her tongue out at him.

From then on, things were different. Oh, Kata's father was still mean, but her fairy godmother froze him each time and Kata always got to say and do whatever she needed to do.

♋

The Key

By DIANA Z.

Once upon a time there was a very little girl. She was a gentle child, with a kind and loving heart. But she lived in a very unkind, brutal place where gentleness was seen as a weakness and was preyed upon by the hunters, and kindness was scoffed at and made the child more vulnerable to attacks by the stalkers. Being so young, she didn't know about anger, hatred and prevailing anarchy or how to protect herself from it. She only knew that she wanted to feel safe, and she wanted to love, and needed to be loved in return.

She reached out to those within her reach, only to find that they had the killer instincts of the hunters, not the love and warmth she needed badly. Time after time, she reached out with her heart, hoping that she would feel the love she needed and have her love and gentleness accepted instead of turned away or trampled. But instead, her love was used against her. And each time she was conquered, squelched and tossed aside, a little bit of her heart was torn away and she was left bleeding and confused. Why wouldn't they love her? What was wrong with her? She couldn't figure out how to make it different.

She did not know that even though she had a loving and generous heart, she was destined to be ridiculed and destroyed by these people. They did not understand love and they could not return it. Slowly, from living in so much pain, the girl began to lose faith that there was love available to her; that there was even love in the world. She began to believe that all people were vicious and unloving and wanted only to hurt her. She learned painful lessons about the absence of love and the anguish of being alone.

Each time her heart was trampled and her love turned away, a little bit of her heart withered and died. Her broken and starved heart was dying from wounds; too prolonged, numerous, and sustained. She realized she had just enough to stay alive, if she could hide her heart away where no one could get to it and hurt her anymore. So the girl began to withdraw, putting up a facade that would hide her real self.

She began to dig a moat encircling her heart — deep, with turbulent waters and many hazards and eddies, that only the courageous could cross. Then she began to build a wall around her heart; a strong, tall edifice that the hunters could not penetrate nor scale. It had many facets of protection and mystery that baffled the hunters and kept them at bay. It was an everchanging wall, sometimes soft,but hard as nails, aloof and elusive. It seemed to have no way in and yet at times seemed as if it did not exist.

The hunters looked and sometimes saw nothing and yet they could not get in. Many scratched their heads and walked away. Those who stayed and tried to conquer her could only shoot arrows over the wall in hopes of wounding her. Sometimes, their arrows found their mark and she was left hurting, but they could no longer see the proof of their work and soon lost interest and left, searching for weaker game. To others it appeared a dark and foreboding place and not at all appealing to explore or possess.

She was such a young girl to build such a strong fortress. But she had little choice if she was to survive. Besides, she had been clever to build such a strong wall to protect her while she nursed her dying heart. Now she was safer, less afraid of dying at their hands. They could still wound her every now and then , but they could not kill her.

But even as she felt safer, she felt very alone. She still had a loving and generous heart and she still needed to be loved as much as she had before. Being alone at such an early age is difficult, even if it was her choice. As she was building the wall, intent on surviving, she hadn't realized that she could not heal her heart alone. She knew she needed to be loved to heal, but she did not know how to do this for herself. She knew she desperately needed to be able to love others in return, but now she was all alone. She had spent all this time fortifying her safety, when in reality she was sealing her fate. She wasn't bleeding quite so badly, but she was far from healed.

So the girl resolved to build a secret door which would have magical powers. It could be seen only by loving hearts, but even they could not get through the door without the key. Those who forded the waters but held malice for her in their hearts would see only a solid, formidable wall that stood strong against their attacks while she hid behind the safety of the stone.

The girl worked hard at the door, a scary and courageous choice. When finished, it would be a beautifully detailed creation. Each detail, if deciphered, would tell the story of her life. It would hold her hopes, fears, and deepest dreams. It would hold her pain, sorrow and loneliness. It too would be elusive and changing, but always true to her heart and her dreams.

But as the girl worked on the door, her fear came to haunt her. What if some hearts could fool the door and hid malice in their hearts to be unleashed after they achieved her trust? What if love was an illusion and no one would ever come? What if she was too afraid to give the key to anyone and was left alone to die from sorrow and pain? She tried hard to put her fears aside and have faith. She just worked harder and poured her hopes into the door.

After the door was complete, she began to work on the key for the lock. She fashioned the key out of grains of hope and the steel of her convictions. She polished it to a deep resolve and hung it around her neck, close to her wounded heart. All she could do now was wait and hope.

After many days and years of waiting, she began to lose hope that anyone had a gentle heart like hers. She began to believe anew what the hunters had lived and instilled in her. She believed that love was an illusion and trust held only pain. The key was a constant reminder of her prison.

Then one day quite by surprise, as the girl walked along the top of the wall surveying the surroundings, she saw someone standing at the door. She was astounded. She blinked her eyes and looked again. Maybe she wanted it so badly that she was wishing it to be. But still, there stood a person studying the door. This person had crossed the treacherous waters, and could see the door!

The girl stood trembling. Could it be that right before her, just on the other side of her treasured door, stood a person with a true and loving heart? What should she do now? Her first instinct was to run; to hide in her strong fortress and wait for the person to go away. Everyone eventually loses interest. Now that the time had come, she was afraid to trust her magical door.

She felt suddenly afraid and unsure of what to do next. When she had built the door she hadn't realized how much risk she was taking. She had never encountered this before and she had sublimely assumed that when the time came, she could do it with ease and anticipation. After all, if one waits a year for a drink, they would gulp down one offered them, wouldn't they? So why was she hesitating? Then she remembered all the stored-up pain she had carried for so long and she knew why she was afraid. No one had ever been safe before and she was terrified of trusting her magic door to know a loving heart when it saw one.

So, she pulled herself in, clutched the key at her heart and hid in her fortress, waiting for the person to leave. But instead of leaving, the person sat down quietly by the door and studied the carvings so

lovingly chiseled into the solid wood. There were many sad sorrow-
ful tales of the girl's life, for those who could see them, and the girl
became even more afraid of how much she had exposed on her
enchanted door.

She ran to the top of her wall, as far away from the person as she
could get, and timidly called down, "What do you want?"

The person looked up and smiled. This frightened the girl even
more. She could see her. The girl spread her arms across her chest,
pumped up her courage, put on her meanest look and said, "What
do you want? Why are you here?"

"It's a beautiful door. It came from loving hands."

The girl felt very afraid. This person could see her and her magic
door! She had tried everything she could think of to drive the person
away. She had put on her nastiest face, insulted the person and made
every effort to drive the kind one out, but still she remained. The girl
walkedaway from the wall trembling with fear and uncertainty and
hid again inside her f o r t r e s s.

But the war within her would not allow her to hide forever. She
didn't know what to do, but she knew she didn't want to be alone
any longer. Her heart had been alone for so long, and she could not
heal it by herself.

She began to question her choice. Had she done the right thing?
What if it was a caring person? How would she know unless she
tried? She crept to the edge of the wall again and peered over the side,
half-hoping the person had decided she wasn't worth the effort. But
much to her fear and surprise, the person was sitting, quietly waiting.

She was astounded. She had used the best tools she had to push
people away. She had even tried ones she had seen used by the
hunters, but nothing had worked. This person stayed, seemingly
waiting for her to make the next move. The person wasn't trying to
scale the wall or shoot arrows to harm her. There was quiet and
patience and the girl was very confused.

She paced back and forth, trying in desperation to figure this
out. It was all new for her. She thought that when the time came,
she would know what to do. She would feel inside herself that this
was right and safe. But all she felt now was fear, horribly heavy,
anguishing fear and doubt. How could she let someone inside her
fortified sanctuary? How could she trust when she had never really
trusted before? How could she let another person see her pain without waiting for more pain? Trust was too scary and unknown...a
dream. There, too, was fear that embracing this goodness would
cause more hurt to surface and her wounded heart felt too weak for

more pain.

She clutched the key at her heart and wondered what good the door was if she could not use it to free herself. She swallowed back tears of frustration. She took a deep breath, hurried down the stairs and went to the door. Standing there, she used one of the door's magical powers and looked hazily through it at the one sitting on the other side. The person did not seem like a hunter or a stalker. She did not seem to even carry a weapon, but the girl knew that words can wound as deeply as arrows and require no cartage. The face seemed free of veils and camouflage. The door recognized a true and loving heart. But, how could she know for sure?

The tears began to flow more freely as her frustration and fear mounted. What more did she need? She had the chance she had wished and prayed for sitting just on the other side of her beautiful and steadfast door. What else need she do? How could she truly trust? How could she hand over the key she had hidden against her wounded heart for so long? The choice was there, right there within her grasp. The rest was up to her.

She heard the person talking to her now, a pleasant voice and a calm manner, but the girl's anxiety was screaming for safety, and solitude was the reply. Her fear overcame her and she wept bitter tears. She suddenly realized that the safety of her fortress had become a prison and she did not know how to break free.

She asked herself again, what more did she need to reach out and let someone in? What needed to change before she could do this scary and courageous thing? Then she realized that nothing more could be offered. Someone had forded the treacherous waters and looked kindly upon the door and even saw the girl's pain. The door saw and recognized her. Nothing more could be done to prove this heart to be true and loving. Only trust would bear out the truth.

Courage was the only thing that would help her now. Even through her fear and her justified wariness, courage was the only solution. Courage alone would give the strength needed to open the door so she could risk closeness and find out if the heart before her was indeed true and loving.

She reached for the key at her chest and tore it from her neck. She held it in her hand. It felt warm. Its warmth gave her promise and hope. She wondered what to do next. She knew she would have to act fast before her courage failed her. She was afraid to throw the key from the wall for fear it would fall into the moat and be lost. There was only one key and she would have only one chance. Her arms were not long enough to reach and no ladder could traverse the wall.

She cried more tears; tears of frustration and futility. She had built the wall too strongly. She had not foreseen the risk of locking her heart away so carefully. Her tears began to flow so heavily that the ground began to soften. The gathering tears rose to her ankles and brought more tears in their wake. The flood gates on her stored-up pain began to give way from the strain of grief bridled too long. The tears seeped into the foundation of her mighty fort and pushed their way out through a tiny crack in a seam. The mortar gave up its hold and one lone brick tumbled from her wall. She heard the rush of tears as they poured through the opening.

She was struck with fear at the loss of her safety. The door and key were forgotten as she began to work furiously to repair the wall. She grabbed a brick and quickly mixed the mortar. But even in her haste, the flow of tears did not cease.Each time she bent over to drive the brick in place and force the mortar into the cracks, the tears fell into the cement, diluting it and ruining its ability to seal her in. After a third try, she stopped and sat down in defeat to cry her tears.

As she sat crying, she heard a small voice inside her say, "This is your chance. Pass the key through the hole. I don't want to be alone anymore." She looked down at the key, still clutched in her hand, and remembered her aloneness. She opened her palm, reached for the opening, and dropped the key to the cold stone. She stood and looked at the wall. She could see another crack in the mortar of her fortress. She reached up and pushed at the brick and it fell to the ground. She looked through the opening, tears streaming from her face, and hoped that she would not have to be alone any longer. She could only hope that this true and loving heart would know what to do with the key and would not be afraid of her pain.

The End
(and the beginning)

♋

The Metamorphosis

By STEPHANIE EICHEL

The caterpillar stirs, so slightly, from within his constricting abode, his shackles binding...stifling. He considers his former state: crawling close, almost clinging to the ground, eating debris, never realizing that above his head flies the butterfly, free to explore the heights.

But there comes a time when he can no longer be bound, and he is released to experience the unlimited freedom of which he had no previous knowledge.

I, too, crawled in the dust, and not so long ago. And from within the ties that bind me to my former days, there is a ray of hope. In time, my shackles will no longer bind, and I will evolve, emerge, and be exposed to a life that I knew could exist for me if only I could be released from the status of mere survival. My colors will be beautiful, kaleidoscopic. You may not recognize me, unless perhaps you have stolen a glimpse of my imminent transformation as it unfolds within my chains.

I wait in anticipation for the metamorphosis.

♋

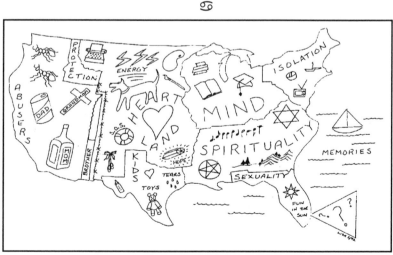

My country.
By B.D.

Robin's Story

By ROBIN

(Dedicated to Jan)

Once there was a grownup named Robin. She was quite mature and sophisticated on the outside. You see, she had learned well how to pretend and put on a mask, even though she had never gone to acting school. Just about everybody who knew her thought she was good and noble and kind and mature. And although that was true, that was only on the outside. Grownup Robin knew something was terribly wrong on the inside because each time she was good or noble or kind or mature, it hurt inside and she lost a little more strength. She didn't know what was wrong.

If her friends could have looked on the inside, they wouldn't have believed what they saw. In fact, when Robin looked on the inside, she didn't believe it either. There was no mask, no sophistication. There was only this small, small child huddled in the corner. Sometimes the child would sigh deeply and catch her breath, as if she had been crying. And her eyes were a bit puffy, and her face was streaked and blotchy. She was leaning against the wall resting, but you just knew she wasn't very comfortable.

If you watched her closely and for a long time, you could see she was shivering, but almost invisibly as if coming from deep inside, and not any cold outside. Sometimes she would tug at her socks, or pull down on her skirt as if to cover and protect more of herself.

Sometimes her mouth would move as if she were sucking on a peppermint, but nothing was there. And she would stroke her hair for comfort. But mostly she would hold herself tight in a very small position as if to take up the smallest possible space.

The only other thing in this inside space was a mirror, dirty, with jagged edges, like what you might find in the dump. It was a magical mirror, for it did not simply reflect what was before it. Instead, the person who looked in it saw what they had learned to see.

Small Robin did not know this was a magical mirror. She only knew that mirrors were supposed to reflect the truth. So that even if she could have seen beyond the dirt and filth that was on the mirror, she would not have seen the delicately pretty little girl that she was. She wouldn't have been able to see the intelligent eyes, the sometimes impish, sometimes innocent smile, the strong arms and legs ready to conquer the world, or the hands eager to help or play. No, she didn't see any of this.

What small Robin did see was even stranger than the magic of the mirror, for she saw different things at different times. Sometimes she saw people who were quite worldly and grown up. You could tell who they were because they used big words and could talk to people, and sipped wine with their pinky in the air. Some were real funny or real strong. Mostly she saw small frightened children. One was even deformed.

She was sad when she saw herself, for this must be the truth. These were hard times for her. The hardest times, though, were when she looked in the mirror and saw nothing. She couldn't believe her eyes and frantically tried to wipe away the grime where she should have been. But the mirror just smeared more, and still there was no reflection. Finally she began to believe it. There was no Robin, and she began to wish she too would just disappear forever.

A long time passed, and grownup Robin met a very nice lady named Jan. She was *very* sophisticated and Robin couldn't believe Jan wanted to be her friend. (Robin was impressed by sophistication.) They spent a lot of time talking and Jan kept on asking if she could come close and look inside. You see, Jan liked Robin and already knew that the real treasure of a person was on the inside. Robin didn't know exactly what was on the inside, except that she knew it was bad and ugly. Who would want to look inside, and why? She was *very* suspicious. No, it couldn't be done. Jan was nice and all, but there are limits.

But you see, Jan understood about mirrors because she had dared to look in her own mirror and so finally to see her true reflection. She was so smart and wise that she just knew that there must be a distorted magical mirror in Robin, if she could only get Robin to trust her to go inside. You see, she understood the magic of the mirrors and how to fix it.

So they continued to talk. And little by little Robin began to trust Jan and let her inside.

When finally Jan got inside, and saw the beautiful but sad little girl, and saw the dirty, jagged mirror, she knew exactly what needed to be done. But first, she stooped down so as not to scare small Robin, and took the sad, frightened child in her arms. They stayed in that position a long time with Jan softly murmuring to her that she was there to comfort and to help, and that small Robin needn't be afraid, but to rest. When small Robin was quiet and able to relax, she stood aside and let Jan begin work on the mirror.

Jan felt so badly for small Robin seeing the dirty, jagged mirror. She knew how hurt, injured and confused small Robin must be, and how painful her past must have been to have such a dirty and jagged mirror, and she longed to be able to help straighten the mirror.

With supplies she brought for this purpose Jan first cleaned off the mirror, then laboriously chiseled away at the jagged edges of the mirror to give it a smooth and uniform shape. She knew this would take the magic away from the mirror, and allow small Robin to see herself clearly and in truth. This was hard work. What needed to be done was straightforward enough, but there were little crevices and chinks that hid more dirt and rough edges.

If it were only the crevices and chinks it still would have been comparatively easy, but small Robin began to panic. As much as the mirror pained her, that was all she possessed. Was Jan trying to take even that away from her?

Poor Jan! Her muscles ached from working on the mirror and now small Robin was trying to push her away. If only she could get it done quickly, then small Robin could see and understand. She was bigger than small Robin and certainly could have gone on working, but she saw the panic in small Robin's eyes. So she stopped and enveloped small Robin in her arms and soothed her and explained what she was doing and so comforted her.

Small Robin loved these times and took strength from them and allowed Jan to go on working. But every now and then Jan would stop and she was glad to hold small Robin, and they would talk and they would both get strength from these times.

Finally the day came when the mirror had no more crevices or jagged edges. It was so smooth you could run your finger around the edge and not get cut. It didn't even need a frame. Jan gave it a final polish so that its sparkle was as clear as spring air after a rain. Then she led small Robin to the mirror. This was the part Jan enjoyed most.

In Jan's arms, small Robin looked in the mirror. She searched for the familiar faces. She was confused, and at first couldn't understand the changed mirror, or rather, the changed reflection.

Jan delighted to show the new small Robin in the mirror. Small Robin could still see all the other people — the funny, angry, sophisticated, small others. But there were two big differences. As time went on she realized there was always someone looking back at her. She never didn't see anyone. She really did exist! And the others now took on a sort of transparent quality, as if the features of each were individually transposed onto herself, the solid figure. At first she saw each individually with her, but the more she looked, and the more Jan encouraged (and yes, talked some more), they began to all be together on her, so that you couldn't tell any of them apart. They were all now a part of her.

And then, as if this weren't enough, as Jan continued to encourage, and as small Robin continued to peer into the mirror, it was as if she were absorbing the wonderful words as her own and into herself, for she began to grow and grow until finally she grew right into grown-up Robin and they were one. Now grownup Robin could be funny and sophisticated and angry and happy and smart and play with dolls and go to concerts and enjoy all good things big and small, and sometimes be sad, but never again lonely, because she was whole.

People should always have fun.
By Sue K.

Our Christmas Tree

By MARY R.

Mary stood in front of a one-story house with a puzzled expression on her face and a key to the front door in her left hand. "I guess this is the one — it's the correct address," she said to herself. "I still can't believe I'm doing this." As she shivered in the cold, Mary looked around and noticed that the sun had just set and Venus was visible. "I guess it's time to go inside now," she said, putting the key in the lock and opening the door.

The house was uninhabited. She walked into the living room, empty except for an armchair and an undecorated Christmas tree, and sat down in the chair. She glared at the tree, a fragrant pine, then looked once again at the piece of paper in her right hand.

In Mary's own sloppy handwriting, the paper read: *Therapy homework: My homework for group is to decorate the Christmas tree in the house at 3627 Maple Ave., which just happens to be newly built and unoccupied. The house contains a kitchen, dining room, living room, three bedrooms, and a bathroom. I will find everything I need to complete this assignment inside the house, and I have to pay close attention to the way the rooms are arranged and make sure to keep good records of what I find.* "Well," decided Mary, "I can't say that I understand this, but I guess it's time to get started. What do you guys think?"

Mary felt a surge of fear as she realized that no one was answering her. "Sheila? Jessica? Katie? Alexandra? Nancy? Mary Gators? Samantha? Anybody else? Where are all of you? Can anyone answer me?"

Silence.

Well, that's just great, Mary thought. *I don't know if they are asleep or just not answering, but I guess I'm on my own. Sometimes being a multiple and having co-consciousness really bothers me, but I don't think that being one person is what it's cracked up to be. I'm not one person yet, but I feel really lonely now that I can't hear or speak with anyone else. I hope they come back soon.*

Mary looked at the tree. "Well, tree, I guess it's just you and me. Do you have a name?" she said out loud.

The tree did not answer.

"No, I guess you won't talk to me either. Well, I'm supposed to decorate you, so here we go! There's no time like the present — ha ha! I don't see any decorations in here, so I will look around the house. Since this is my homework, I'm sure there is some way to get it done."

A quick glance around the living room revealed its lack of decorations. *I'll try the dining room first*, Mary decided. She immediately noticed a group of animal-shaped ceramic ornaments on the dining room table. Picking up a bunny she spoke aloud, "Oh, Sheila would love this. Sheila? Can you hear me?"

No response.

I wonder what she's up to, Mary thought. *I guess she's being sneaky. Well, I'm supposed to keep good records, so here goes.* She wrote *dining room* on her piece of paper and added *bunny ornament* underneath it. Among the other ornaments were a kitten, a duck, a bird, Snoopy, Elmo, Big Bird, and Cookie Monster. "Now wait a minute," Mary cried, "This is just a little *too* coincidental. All of these animal ornaments just *happen* to be perfect for the kids? The tree has something to do with *us* and I'm supposed to figure it out! *That's* why no one has been talking to me since I got here! Well, you guys, I'll figure this one out in no time, even if I can't rely on Miss Brilliant Jessica to help me !"

Mary listed the animal ornaments and the names of the appropriate personalities on the piece of paper and then took the ornaments and carefully hung them on the tree. She walked back into the dining room and picked up the remaining objects on the table: a rag doll, a green and purple pinwheel, and some Christmas wrapping paper. "This isn't too hard," Mary said. "The rag doll is for little Mary Katherine and the pinwheel is for Mary Kate. And the paper is there for wrapping the presents. At least I assume these are supposed to be presents." Mary dutifully recorded the items and the names on the paper and decided to try the kitchen next. The table was covered with unwrapped boxes. She opened a large box holding Christmas tree lights underneath a card which said *Mary Rose*. Smiling to herself, Mary said, "This is great! The homework is getting easier all the time!"

Mary put all of the presents in the living room and looked around. No other Christmas-type paraphernalia was in view. She was about to leave the kitchen when she heard a soft sound from outside. Glancing out of a window in the kitchen, she realized that the sound was caused by the rippling of a river which came up to the bottom of a small hill in the backyard of the house.

"Oh, this is beautiful!" Mary exclaimed. "I've got to go outside and sit near the water for a while! I deserve a break from homework anyway." She made sure she still had the front door key and left the house. As Mary walked to the edge of the river, she saw that the moon had risen and was shining on the water. She sat down on the hill near the water and watched the waves become smaller and disappear as they traveled toward the land.

The sight and sound of the water was very relaxing, and Mary felt calm for the first time since she had entered the house. She had not realized how much she depended on the communication with the other parts, and she had really missed talking with everyone else. As Mary was thinking she ought to tell the other parts how much she liked their company, she saw a soda can floating towards her. She picked it up, frowning at this evidence of environmental pollution. She felt as if she'd been cast out to sea and left to float — without the others — like the can. Mary sighed as she realized that her post-integration life would probably be very difficult if she was having this much trouble coping without the other parts right now. For the millionth time, she wondered what "she" would be like after everyone integrated.

Mary sighed. It was time to return to the house. A small mountain of items now sat in the living room, waiting to be arranged in their proper places. Mary began to put the lights on the tree, and finished trimming it, except for the tinsel; she wanted to delay adding the tinsel until she was sure she had found all the ornaments.

Picking up her pen and paper, Mary decided to explore the rest of the house. The bathroom held a card which read "To Geraldine" and a Christmas stocking filled with soap, candy, and perfumes. The first bedroom in the house held presents wrapped in several distinctive styles of paper. Mary picked up a present and unsuccessfully tore at the paper, frowning when she realized that the paper would not come off. "Well, I guess this means something," Mary said.

The locked door to the second bedroom opened with the help of the front door key. Twelve presents sat in the room, wrapped in gold and green paper. Another set of twelve presents wrapped in plain white tissue paper were sitting in a pile below a sign which read "*The Twelve Days of Christmas*." As in the first bedroom, none of the wrappings could be removed; this time, no names identified the proper recipients. Mary sighed, recorded her observations on her trusty piece of paper, and put these presents under the tree with the others.

The door to the third bedroom was locked and could not be opened by any method. "I wonder what's in there?" Mary said. She scribbled a few words on her paper, glanced at her description of the therapy homework, and added a few more phrases as she noticed the house did not have an attic, basement, or laundry room.

Satisfied that there were no other decorations for the tree in the house, Mary added the tinsel to the tree. She smiled to herself: the meaning of the homework was obvious. "The tree symbolizes me," Mary said, ' And the decorations and presents stand for the other parts of us. At first I was alone; however, I then found some parts who were obvious, then some who were more hidden. Others have revealed their names but little else. From my point of view, some are locked away,some are missing, and some are so far away that I don't even know if or when they've gone or where they are! Wow, this is amazing! I've learned a lot about us and a lot about appreciating all of you guys, and not pushing integration! Thanks, everyone!"

It was now quite late at night, and Mary was about ready to doze off to sleep when a sudden instinct made her jerk awake. She quietly opened the front door, stepped outside, and saw several deer munching on grass in a clearing across the street from the house. After a while the deer had eaten their fill and left the clearing.

Mary went back to the living room and sat down, thinking about families. "I'm so glad I saw those deer," she mused. "And I'm glad I have our family of people inside. Thanks, everyone." She dozed off to sleep sitting in the chair, with the Christmas lights forming a multicolored nightlight.

A few hours later, Mary awoke. It was now early morning and time to leave the house. She unplugged the Christmas tree lights, walked out of the house and closed and locked the front door. As she turned towards the street, she saw that the sun was rising in the sky.

Mary sat up and looked around. She was sitting in a chair in her bedroom and she immediately said, "Guys, how are you?" out loud. She laughed with relief when Sheila replied, "I'm O.K. But I want some yummy food. *Now*. And I want Judy Rainbow Bunny." Mary stood up to get the bunny but stopped when she saw the paper in her right hand which read:

Therapy homework: Spend some time meditating on what new things we have accomplished/learned about ourself since we started therapy. Mary felt embarrassed and was about to say, "I hate having a dissociative disorder," when she saw that the paper in her left hand contained the instructions to decorate the tree as well as all of Mary's observations from the "meditation exercise." At the bottom of the paper, Jessica had added:

MARY,

NOTHING THAT EXISTS CAN EVER BE LOST. FOR YOU AND FOR US, WHAT WE FEARED WAS LOST HAS BEEN RE-GAINED. WE STARTED LIFE AS ONE PERSON; SOMEDAY WE WILL BE ONE PERSON AGAIN WHEN WE ARE READY. BUT FOR NOW, BE CONTENT THAT NOW IS A TIME OF NEW BEGIN-NINGS. WE HAVE SPENT OUR LIVES SURVIVING AND ENDURING PAIN. NOW IS OUR TIME TO LIVE.

JESSICA

A world of healing.
By Heather B.

Little Flower

A Story of Survival

By RACHEL OF NANCY

Once upon a time there was a beautiful meadow tucked away high in the heart of a magnificent mountain range. The meadow was serene and perfect in many ways; birds chirped happily, butterflies flitted about, and the life cycle of the meadow continued on peacefully.

In the meadow, many beautiful flowers and wild grasses swayed gently with the breeze. But as with all things, the meadow also had its share of imperfections. Amongst the abundant foliage, some persistent dandelion weeds also grew. A casual glance did not reveal these weeds but if one took the time to savor each minute detail, one could see Dandelions invading the meadow's beauty. Caught in between the two largest Dandelions was a small Flower, struggling to live and add her beauty to the landscape.

But every time Little Flower tried to grow, Dandelions would push it down, choking her roots to prevent her from growing any more. Little Flower knew deep down that life was meant to be good, and knew that if she could get free of the tangled roots of Dandelions, she would become the most magnificent flower in the meadow.

Little Flower did everything she could to grow and spread her beauty — listening as the other Flowers described how happy life could be in the meadow free of Dandelions. But for a long time, the only way Little Flower could survive was to scatter her seeds as far from herself as she could, hoping they would take root and save Little Flower from a sure death.

Meanwhile, Little Flower worked hard to please the Dandelions, hoping that if she could persuade the Dandelions to nurture her growth, that someday she would become stronger than they. Time passed on, and Little Flower, finally rootbound, could grow no more. Then Little Flower listened even more closely to the other flowers and grasses in the meadow. They said that Dandelions were evil weeds that must not be allowed to spread any further.

Little Flower tried to believe this. But she had always been so close to the Dandelions, hearing all the bad things they said, that Little

Flower found it hard to believe she could *ever* be stronger than the Dandelions.

But she did not give up. Instead, as more time passed, Little Flower decided to work harder than she ever had before. With the help and encouragement of all the flowers, she thought long and hard about how to break free of the choking Dandelions. She pushed and pushed through the soil, with all her might, until she became as big as the Dandelions. They became frightened and upset with Little Flower, who had exposed their evil roots which had been safely hidden all these years. Little Flower, also frightened, began to see the possibility of freedom, so again she worked hard to grow stronger. Finally, Little Flower was ready to overcome the Dandelions. She told them all that they had done to prevent her from growing, and that never more would she allow the Dandelions to choke her roots.

Shortly after this, a tremendous rain storm drenched the meadow. Although at first Little Flower believed she would drown from so much water, she discovered that the rain had softened the soil around the Dandelions. With the faith and encouragement of the older, wiser flowers, Little Flower pulled up the Dandelions, roots and all, and flung them into the nearby boulders where their roots could not take hold. She was sad to have to do this, but knew it was the only way that she could begin to thrive.

To this day, the Dandelions still lay on the rocks where they were thrown. They lie there, withered, dry, alone, and dead to any beauty they might once have had.

Little Flower is thriving and becoming the precious flower she was meant to be. She now joins the other meadow flowers in keeping the meadow free from Dandelions, and helps those flowers that get tangled up in them. She now lives peacefully, free from the choking Dandelions forever more.

♋

The Rescue Parade

A story in pictures

By Libby

Before

I

II

III

IV

V

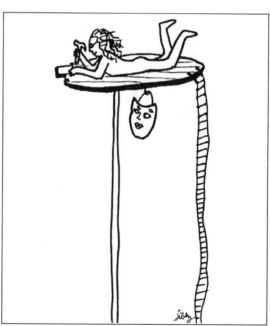

VI

VII

Reflections

By DIANA Z.

Once upon a time, there was a young girl who lived an uncertain life in very uncertain times. She lived in a narrow world of noisy, frightening chaos among angry, hurtful people. From very early on, she carried the pain and scars of the chaos and the crazies who lived among it. She felt little hope and often felt close to giving up.

Amid the turmoil, the best she could do was watch and listen carefully and learn the lessons she needed to survive. She learned to live with anxiety and the uncertainty of her uncertain world. She learned not to question the insanity of the chaos, for it only made her crazy like them and threatened what safety she had learned to imagine. She learned not to challenge the strength of the craziness or the allure of the turmoil that helped keep it in place. She learned the difference between fear and terror and that indifference is almost worse than hatred. For self-preservation, she learned the art of silence, even in pain and heart-wrenching betrayal. She learned to be very small, almost invisible, to hide from the terror and the confusion of the craziness of her world and those she shared her world with...the crazies...the ones who lived the chaos, created the chaos, honed the chaos to a fine art.

Some lessons were very painful and cost her a great deal. Although she hung onto life with a tenacity that showed determination and promise, she lost much of herself along the way in the frantic scramble to survive.

As she grew, she listened carefully. She had no choice if she was to survive. In this land of chaos, this narrow view of life, the girl knew of herself only in terms of how those around her viewed her. She saw what they saw. In their faces she could see herself and it was not a pretty sight. She was an ugly, loathsome, disgusting creature, less than human. She saw a lumbering ogre with an imbecilic countenance. Lazy, ugly, fat, useless, stupid, weak— these were all things she saw of herself in the faces of those around her, and she grew to hate herself and avoided looking at her reflection in their eyes. She spent most of her time alone, for it was safer and did not constantly remind her of the futility of her existence. She was alive, but what good was it? She wasn't worth being alive. She wasn't lovable or worthy. She was a monster and her heart ached and secretly wept from the burden.

Her solitary time gave her the freedom to wander far from the center of the chaos and spared her the jeers bestowed upon her by the ones around her. She roamed through fields and watched birds gliding gracefully through the air, dreaming of freedom from her prison. She learned to let her mind drift and dream of love, even though she didn't think she knew how to recognize it.

Day after day, she slipped away and ventured farther into the unexplored regions of the land, until one day she found a deep forest of tall, sturdy, wise trees that spread their branches as if in greeting. They offered lush cool shade from the heat and unforgiving sun. She stepped into the shelter of the trees and found a new world around her. A magical transformation of sight and smell had brought a dream world to life. She watched the light play among the leaves and delighted in the kaleidoscope of color that performed for her amusement. The trees bent down and offered their beauty to behold. They cooled her with their shade and the rustling leaves seemed to speak in murmurs of anticipation, as if they had been waiting for her.

They parted their branches and appeared to urge her forward, whispering words of pressing import. She followed the path the trees gave her, wondering why they would bother with such a horrible creature as herself. The trail meandered on into the trees and although the thought crossed her mind that she might get lost in the forest, she felt a calm sense of trust in the wise old trees. "Besides," she thought with a shrug, "No one would miss me anyway."

She walked on, growing tired and thirsty, and began to forget why she had embarked on this adventure. As she walked, musing, she began to consider turning back. After all, they were just trees, only good for cutting down and burning. That's what the crazies did with them. They saw no beauty or majesty in their wide spread limbs, only what they could get out of them.

As she walked, she slowly noticed a change in her surroundings; the light filtered more deeply into the foliage. But in spite of that, there was a coolness in the air and the sweet smell of fresh water. She looked ahead and to her delight she saw the sun reflecting brightly from a source beyond her sight. She quickened her step and hurried toward her destiny.

As she broke through the last of the protecting trees, she drew in her breath in astonishment. What she saw was beyond her imagination. It was better than any dream she ever conceived. She had not known such beauty existed in the world.

Hesitantly, she stepped into the realm of this magical place, sat down on the soft grass and began to cry quietly. She did not know why or even how the tears flowed, and she felt weak for their display. The crazies never cried. They called it a weakness. But the beauty around her stirred something deep within the girl, opening her heart.

Through her tears she saw a hushed clearing with trees drawn to the edges as if for protection. Inside the glen, she saw beautiful wildflowers. A sense of peace came over her. Amid the foliage, rabbits and squirrels scurried, playing among themselves, causing her to smile in spite of her tears.

But most striking of all was a peaceful lake that reflected the sun's brilliance. She had never seen a lake before. The land of chaos was dry and barren. She looked at the water and wondered at the feel of it. Would it be hard as it appeared? She moved timidly closer and sat again to study the unknown surface. She could see the trees mirrored on its smooth sheen. She jumped, astonished to see birds flying in the water! How could birds fly in water? They fly free in the air. She looked up at the sky and to her surprise, there were indeed birds gliding in the air above the lake. She looked back at the lake and laughed, even though laughter was forbidden, for she saw the birds were not in the water at all, but reflected on the lake's surface as the trees were.

On her hands and knees, she moved close enough to the lake to touch it. She reached one finger forward, timorously touched the surface and jumped back in apprehension. But to her delight, it was soft and cool. Waves rippled out from the place where her finger disturbed the water, and she watched as the lake acknowledged her presence with serene acceptance. The water was so cool and her feet so tired from the trek that she sat down, removed her shoes and silently slipped her feet into the water. She almost recoiled from the overwhelming sensation the water's embrace brought to her senses. She had never known a quiet, calm embrace; only angry, painful attacks.

Once more she began to cry softly. This unexpected gentleness had crept into her inner world and caused feelings she had never known: feelings of longing for gentleness and ease from her pain. Lost in her sorrow, she did not hear the voice at first. But as the voice was close and unmistakably gentle, and accompanied by a soft poking of her feet, it finally was heard past the girl's anguish.

The sound so startled the girl that she forgot her tears and looked up to see where the voice came from. Then she remembered herself and tried to hide her features, lest the person run from fright or disgust upon seeing the hideous mask that was her face.

Again she heard the voice, soft and melodic, gently probing for a response. "My hello is not so frightening, is it?" said the hushed voice.

"No," was the only reply the girl could push past the lump in her throat.

"Then why do you hide your face?" asked the voice.

"Because I am a hideous creature. No one can look upon me without disgust. I do not want to leave this place, and you will surely insist I leave if you see me."

All the girl heard in return was a gentle laugh, a tinkling really, like water dancing over pebbles in a stream. The girl looked up in surprise, wondering at the person who could laugh at such horrible ugliness.

"I have seen you already and I see only a young girl full of sorrow and pain. I see no monster."

The girl jerked her head up in surprise and said, "How could you see me? I saw no one here before. Where were you hiding?"

"I saw you as I see the trees and the birds in the sky."

Then suddenly the girl understood. The voice was from the water. She peeked at the water and asked, "You live in the water, then?"

"No, I am the water, the living mirror of life. I have waited a long time for you."

"You? You have waited for me? How do you know me?" the girl stammered.

"Yes, I have waited for you. I have heard your sorrow on the wind and in the tears of the birds who swim in my waters and cry for your suffering. My depths have been deepened by your pain and needless torment."

"The birds cry for me? I didn't even know the birds knew me. They always fly away when I approach. I thought they flew away because I was hideous."

"No, dear child. You do not know your beauty, for you have never seen it."

"Me, beautiful?" Now it was the girl's turn to laugh in spite of herself. How absurd that anyone would use such a word to describe anything about her. She uncovered her face and said to the water, with a hint of sadness and resignation, "Look at me. How can you call this Beauty?"

"It is not difficult to call beauty by its name if your eyes have not been clouded by lies. I reflect only that which is placed before me, and I see only the truth. Do you call the birds ugly or lacking in grace?

Do you call the trees gnarled and hideous?"

The girl could only shake her head.

"Then how can you call yourself ugly or horrible?"

"It is what I have always been," replied the girl.

"Then it is time to see the truth. Look into my eyes and see your face as I see it."

The girl recoiled in horror. She had seen enough of herself reflected in the faces of those in chaos. She could not possibly stand to see herself stripped to the truth. Her first instinct was to run.

She crossed the small meadow heading away from the lake and was near the edge of the trees when she stopped and slowly turned back toward the water. Something held her in check.

Unknown to her, long ago she had tucked away, deep in her heart, a soft, warm place: fertile ground for the planting of a seed of hope. She had protected the tiny grain of her essence, sheltered from the barbs of the crazies. And now, in the midst of this quiet, tranquil place, challenged by the wise waters, her hope began to push its way through the secret paths in her heart out into her waking world.

"I don't understand," was all the girl could manage to say.

"Truth is hard to understand or trust when lies have been your reality. Chaos does not know truth, only deception to maintain its seduction. They lied to you. I see no horrid creature, but a living, breathing, lovable human being. I am not afraid to look upon you or to hold you in your pain. Come. Look upon yourself for the first time. It is only your reflection, nothing more. See what loving and truthful eyes can see."

The girl timidly approached the edge of the lake and sat again near the shore of the rippling water. She wondered if what she was hearing was really true. All her life she had seen herself reflected in the faces around her and they had all seen a hideous creature. How could they all be wrong? Could so much hatred exist in the world? Then she remembered all her stored-up pain and knew that life could indeed hold great cruelty.

She took a deep breath and said to the waters, "All right, I will try. But, what if you see what they saw?"

"My heart sees your beauty. Nothing will change that."

So once more the girl crept toward the edge of the water. She leaned over the calm mirrored surface and dared to look upon her image. Before her eyes, she saw a little girl, no monster or hideous creature. She saw dimples and blond hair and a wide-eyed look of amazement. The picture began to blur as her eyes filled with tears and began to spill over, falling into the waters of the wise lake. She fell back against the grass, stunned by what she had seen.

How could this be true? Could this really be what they called the face of a monster? The lies she had lived with began to crumble. The girl could only rest on the cool grass and sob. Could this image really, truly be what she had always been?

Her sobs increased. Now the girl was lost in her grief and sorrow for the lost years and lost hope.

"Can you swim?" the girl heard through her sobs. She could only shake her head through the tears and grieve her loss.

"Come into the cool waters. I will hold you and allow no harm to come to you. You can rest and weep your weep until you have strength to go on."

The girl now could see the truth of the waters. She silently stepped into the lake in trust, and lay back against its calming support, and cried for what seemed forever. But pain will pass when felt to its depth. The calm lake was a safe refuge. It held her and listened to her anguish and received her tears with reverence and respect. No words were spoken. None were needed.

As the tears flowed freely, her heart began to lighten. She started to think about her life and what was ahead for her.

"What can I do now?" she said to the waters. "I don't want to go back to the land of chaos. They hate me there. I have no hope or life there."

The waters replied softly, "There is life beyond chaos. You have found the edge of a new beginning. You need only gather your strength and venture forward. You do not need them or their chaos or their lies to define your reality. You have your own truth within you."

The girl lay in the water and felt the soft, warm comfort of the lake. In her deepest pain, it had held her and honored her suffering— listening to her grief and seeing her true spirit. This was someone she could believe in.

The seed of hope, forgotten in her mourning, was still growing and now the girl could feel its presence. It gave her strength and a small grain of promise. Yes, there was life beyond chaos. She could live without them.

Now she would find her own truth, her own life...her own beauty.

Integration: A.,B., & E.
By Sherry

Chapter

7

Afterglow

Living in the light

To My Sisters

By HANNA

Dear Sisters of MV

How wonderful to have each of you. To share with and to remember and think about.

I've wanted to share these few lines with someone who would understand. I have shared them with others, but they didn't know. I didn't either. Actually, I wrote these lines maybe three years ago, well before my MPD diagnosis:

> I am me — more
> whole than I feel
> now — more complete
> than I can envision
> why — because I can't
> remember the bulk of
> what completes me or
> fills the emptiness.

Now it makes sense to me, considering all that is inside! If it is a comfort to anyone else, I'm 52 years old and finally am at peace with myself(ves). Feeling as though there are no more surprises. No black monsters yet to come. No heaviness in my mind. No blackness, waiting to engulf me, shutting out the light. There was so much fear associated with all that. Now there is no more fear. Surprises? Maybe not that either. I don't know. But I'm in a good place. I'm confident. I'm more quiet inside than ever before.

Thanks for listening.

Hanna

♋

Warmth

I have felt the warmth
of the light on my fingertips
But I cautiously withdraw
Afraid of the risk
Afraid not to try
So brief is the gentle
moment of acceptance
Then lured by
mesmerizing voices
Into the familiar
comfort of a
wounded spirit
Bound eternally
by this destiny
But I have felt the
warmth of the light

By Cin

♋

Explorer I

Old pleasures re-experienced,
skills I thought forgotten,
joys I believed outgrown,
I explore them all now
without fear of judgment
or laughter.
Writing at midnight.
Drawing only for my satisfaction.
Mixing my own herb teas.
Creating my own jewelry.
Designing greeting cards,
just for fun.
Needing no one's permission
to explore
what brings joy.
How bound and suppressed
I have been
by my need
for others' approval.
How simpler,
more pleasurable,
to only need
my
approval of me.
There are yet worlds to be explored —
I have only begun.

By Daile

♋

Coming Home to Self

BY STEPHANIE EICHEL

I'm home.

I haven't been here in a long time. There are cobwebs and empty cabinets.

I sit on the sofa and gaze through the window at the snow. The blustery wind whips the snow into swirls of whipped topping.

With a chill, I recall the treacherous journey — the hunger, fear, pain, numbness, the enemies encountered along the way, striving with all the energy they could muster to thwart me. At times, I stumbled across the wrong path, my visibility minimal, due to the storm.

Many times, I slept in abandoned shacks, losing all hope of ever reaching my destination alive. But I trudged on. Overcome with weariness and desperation, I doubted myself. Did I have a home? I turned against myself, and the possibility of rescue seemed remote.

But I found my way. I had help; I'm not so proud that I would take all the credit. But in the end it was I who saw the chimney, the smoke.

Now I am safe. I turn from the window and to the fire crackling in the fireplace. It warms the whole room.

Who started the fire? I did, when I refused to think of my trip as a lost cause and found the road leading home. I felt the warmth inside of me, and it spurred me on.

I walk to the cupboard and pull out two crystal goblets. I fill them with grape juice and toast myself.

♋

A Poem for Survivors

In remembrance of you
I light this day
a candle
burning brightly
and without fear
shadows chased away
by innocent smiles
and the night before Christmas

In remembrance of you
I light this day
a candle
burning brightly
and without shame
lighting the path for survivors
of the ritualistic torture
of physical
sexual
and verbal abuse
inflicted on their bodies and souls
in endless hours
of mindnumbing pain

In remembrance of you
I light this day
a candle
burning brightly
and without judgment
erasing in its glow
the voices of those
who would condemn
the troubled journey of a woman
seeking a God
who offers more than just platitudes
and unkept promises

In remembrance of you
I light this day
a candle
burning brightly
and without pain
shining in the eyes

of a child
bursting with joy
as she gazes in wonder
at the Christmas tree
etching forever in memory
the magic of that moment

In remembrance of you
I light this day
a candle
burning brightly
and with tears
dedicated
to keeping alive
the memory
of the terrible struggle
and the price paid
by all those who stood together
to keep the flames
of peace, justice
and hope
from being extinguished

In remembrance of you
I light this day
a candle
burning brightly
and with hope
a shining reminder
of a lasting commitment
to the hidden butterflies
wounded and scarred
still buried in cocoons
of pain and silence
waiting
to catch the first rays
of freedom

In remembrance of you
I light this day
a candle
burning brightly
and without fear...

By Janice S.

Emerging Whole.
By Daile

Resources

Other publications by MANY VOICES PRESS (MV CO.) include:

MANY VOICES
Words of Hope for People with a Dissociative Disorder
Bimonthly, international newsletter. Since 1989, a positive force for healing and sharing among people with Dissociative Identity Disorder (previously known as MPD) and other dissociative conditions. Write or call for current pricing:
PO Box 2639, Cincinnati, OH 45201-2639 (513)531-5415.

MANY VOICES/MULTIPLE CHOICES
By the Staff of *MANY VOICES*
Annual Resource Guide contains listings of health care providers, books, newsletters, etc. Features Survivor Ads (free) which offer services and products sold by survivors to the recovery community. Free to *MANY VOICES* subscribers. Nominal fee to others. Write or call for details: PO Box 2639. Cincinnati, OH 45201-2639. (513)531-5415.

Readers of *MANY VOICES* were also the primary contributors to the prize-winning book **Multiple Personality Disorder From the Inside Out.** Edited by Barry Cohen, Esther Giller and Lynn W. 1991. Published by Sidran Press, 2328 W. Joppa Rd., Suite 15, Lutherville, MD 21093

BOOKS

Several books (such as **Courage To Heal**) are mentioned elsewhere in **Mending Ourselves**. Rather than repeat those worthy publications here, we'd like to add a few others:

Allies in Healing
By Laura Davis. 1991. HarperPerennial,Div HarperCollins Publishers, NY. An excellent guide for partners and non-abusive family members of abuse survivors.

I

United We Stand: A Book for People with Multiple Personalities. By Eliana Gil, Ph.D. Launch Press, P.O. Box 5629, Rockville, MD 20855.

Secret Survivors: Uncovering Incest and Its Aftereffects in Women. By E. Sue Blume. 1990. John Wiley & Sons, NY. Includes incest survivors' checklist. Now available in paperback.

Triumph Over Darkness: Understanding and Healing the Trauma of Childhood Sexual Abuse. By Wendy Ann Wood, M.A. 1993. Published by Beyond Words Publishing Inc. 13950 NW Pumpkin Ridge Rd., Hillsboro, OR 97123.

Managing Ourselves: Building a Community of Caring. By Elizabeth Power. Workbook-type tool for survivors. PO Box 2346, Brentwood, TN 37024-2346.

Multiple Personality Gift: A Workbook for You and Your Inside Family. By Jacklyn M. Pia. Real Active Survivor Inc. PO Box 1894, Canyon Country, CA 91386-0894.

BOOKS FOR PROFESSIONALS

Treatment of Multiple Personality Disorder. By Bennett Braun, M.D.,1986. American Psychiatric Press, 1400 K Street NW,Suite 1101, Washington, DC 20005.

Childhood Antecedents of Multiple Personality.
By Richard Kluft,M.D.,1985. American Psychiatric Press, 1400 K Street NW,Suite 1101, Washington, DC 20005

Multiple Personality Disorder: Diagnosis, Clinical Features, and Treatment. By Colin A. Ross, M.D. , 1989. John Wiley & Sons, NY.

Diagnosis & Treatment of Multiple Personality Disorder,1989.By Frank W. Putnam, M.D., Guilford Publications Inc., NY.

Bibliographies of Professional Articles, Etc.

Multiple Personality, Dissociative States and Traumatic Stress Disorders: A Bibliography for Additional Reading. Edited by Moshe S. Torem, M.D., Akron General Medical Center Dept. of Psychiatry, 400 Wabash Ave. Akron OH 44307 or call 216/384-6525.

Multiple Personality and Dissociation, 1791-1990: A Complete Bibliography. By Carole Goettman, B.A., George B.Greaves, Ph.D., and Philip M. Coons, M.D., 1991. Inquiries to G.B. Greaves, Ph.D. 529 Pharr Rd., Atlanta, GA 30305.

For expanded booklists on topics related to dissociation, child abuse, and incest write to:

American Psychiatric Press, 1400 K Street NW, Suite 1101, Washington, DC 20005

Guilford Publications, Inc. 72 Spring St., New York, NY 10012.

Launch Press, PO Box 5629, Rockville, MD 20855.

Monarch Resources, PO Box 1293, Torrance, CA 90505-0293.

R & E Publishers, PO Box 2008, Saratoga, CA 95070.

John Wiley & Sons, 605 Third Ave., New York, NY 10158-0012.

Stern's Book Service, 2004 W. Roscoe St., Chicago, IL 60618.

Step'N Stones, 1327 C Post Ave., Torrance, CA 90501.

The Sidran Foundation Bookshelf,2328 W. Joppa Rd., Suite 15, Lutherville, MD 21093.

NEWSLETTERS

Body Memories. Radical Perspectives on Child Sexual Abuse. PO Box 14941, Berkeley,CA 94701.

Survivorship. For survivors of ritualized abuse. 3181 Mission St. #139. San Francisco, CA 94110.

Trauma & Recovery Newsletter. Akron General MedicalCenter Dept of Psychiatry. 400 Wabash Ave., Akron,OH 44307.

Treating Abuse Today. Int'l newsjournal of abuse survivorship and therapy. 2272 Eastlake Ave.E.,# 300, Seattle, WA 98102.

AUDIO TAPES

Audio Transcripts Ltd., 335 South Patrick St., Suite 220, Alexandria VA 22314.

ORGANIZATIONS

ISSMP&D:
International Society for the Study of Multiple Personality and Dissociation.
5700 Old Orchard Road, First Floor, Skokie, IL 60077-1057

Believe the Children. , PO Box 26-8462, Chicago, IL 60626.

V.O.I.C.E.S. In Action Inc., PO Box 148309, Chicago, IL 60614.

S.I.A. Survivors of Incest Anonymous, Inc.
PO Box 21817, Baltimore, MD 21222-6817.

Incest Survivors Anonymous.PO Box 5613, Long Beach, CA 90805.

We welcome readers' comments about this book and its resources, so we can keep information up-to-date in future editions. Thank you for caring!

Index Of Contributors